VENTURE INTO A GLOBAL ENTITY

Turn Your Adversities into Success Across Continents

DR. OLAJIDE OKUNROUNMU
Entrepreneur

Copyright © 2024 Dr. Olajide Okunrounmu
All Rights Reserved

Kemp House
152-160 City Road
London, EC1V 2NX
United Kingdom

ISBN 978-1-917451-17-8

Published by Dr. Olajide Okunrounmu and Action Wealth Publishing

Printed and bound in the United Kingdom

This book or any portion thereof may not be reproduced or used in any manner without the express written permission of the publisher except for the use of brief quotations in a book review.

Although the author and publisher have made every effort to ensure the accuracy and completeness of information contained in this book, we assume no responsibility for errors, inaccuracies, omissions, or any inconsistency herein. Any slights on people, places, or organisations are unintentional.

The material in this book is provided for educational purposes only. No responsibility for loss occasioned to any person or corporate body acting or refraining to act as a result of reading material in this book can be accepted by the author or publisher.

Dedicated to my Lord and Savior, Jesus, for the power and mercy you have shown in my life. Without your grace, I would be lost.

TABLE OF CONTENTS

ACKNOWLEDGMENTS _____ 8
PREFACE _____ 11
INTRODUCTION _____ 13
PART 1: AFRICA: MY ROOTS AND FOUNDATIONS 17
CHAPTER 1: SETTING THE STAGE FOR SUCCESS ___ 19
    Empowering Humanity _____ 19
    Overcoming Adversities _____ 21
    Global Perspective _____ 23
    Inspirations and Motivations _____ 25
    Global Leadership Insights _____ 26
    Conclusion _____ 27
CHAPTER 2: FORMATIVE YEARS AND INFLUENCES 29
    Family Dynamics _____ 30
    Structured Education and Personal Growth ___ 32
    Impact of Catholic Disciplines _____ 33
    Community Engagement _____ 34
    Life in Lagos _____ 34
    The Power of Education _____ 35
    Secondary School Life and Lessons _____ 37
    Initiation Into Leadership Roles _____ 38

Lifelong Learning ___ 39
Early Lessons of Responsibility ___ 41
Global Leadership Insights ___ 46
Conclusion ___ 47
CHAPTER 3: HIGHER EDUCATION AND CAREER DEVELOPMENT ___ 49
Polytechnic Years ___ 49
University of Lagos ___ 51
Studying Physiotherapy ___ 54
Academic Achievements ___ 55
Pro Advancements ___ 57
Building Resilience ___ 61
Overcoming Adversities as Preparation ___ 65
Global Leadership Insights ___ 70
Conclusion ___ 72

PART 2: EUROPE: CROSSING BORDERS AND BREAKING BARRIERS ___ 73
CHAPTER 4: NEW BEGINNINGS IN LONDON ___ 75
Stepping Into the Unknown ___ 75
The Motivation Behind Migration ___ 76
Embracing Change ___ 83
Marriage and Starting a Family ___ 86
Preparing for Another Transition ___ 91
Lessons For Success ___ 96
Global Leadership Insights ___ 99
Conclusion ___ 100

PART 3: USA: EXPANDING TO GLOBAL HORIZONS ___ 103

CHAPTER 5: THE BIG MOVE ___ 105
Starting Anew in Michigan ___ 106
Family Adjustments ___ 110
Break New Ground and Overcome Limitations ___ 113
Pursuing The American Dream ___ 117
Global Leadership Highlights ___ 121
Conclusion ___ 123

CHAPTER 6: FROM A LOCAL TO GLOBAL ENTITY ___ 124
Entrepreneurial Ventures ___ 124
Overcoming Obstacles ___ 128
Business Growth ___ 134
The Creation of OKUNSGLOBAL ___ 138
Blueprint for Global Expansion ___ 139
Global Leadership Insights ___ 143
Conclusion ___ 144

CHAPTER 7: THE IMMIGRANT'S DIARIES ___ 146
The Role of Faith and Personal Values ___ 147
Importance of Family and Relationships ___ 152
Attaining Financial Independence ___ 155
Tips For Aspiring Immigrants ___ 159
Global Leadership Insights ___ 164
Conclusion ___ 165

CHAPTER 8: THE POWER OF MENTORSHIP ___ 167
Role Models as Catalysts for Success ___ 167
Influential Family Members ___ 168

Mentors in Education _____ 169
Professional Mentors _____ 170
Public Figures and Historical Leaders _____ 171
Gaining Wisdom and Skills _____ 173
Mentoring Others _____ 176
Pay It Forward _____ 180
Global Leadership Insights _____ 183
Conclusion _____ 184

PART 4: VISIONARY LEADERSHIP AND FUTURE ASPIRATIONS _____ 187

CHAPTER 9: DEFINING VISIONARY LEADERSHIP _ 189
Characteristics of Visionary Leadership _____ 190
Set Realistic Goals _____ 196
Craft a Vision Statement: _____ 198
How a Leader Can Craft a Vision: _____ 199
Aligning Actions with Visions _____ 200
Benefits to the Leader: _____ 202
Benefits to the Organization or People They Lead: _ 203
Leading With Integrity and Authenticity _____ 204
Defining personal ethics: _____ 206
Components of Defining Personal Ethics: _____ 207
Impact of Defining Personal Ethics for Leaders ____ 207
Authentic Communication: _____ 210
Building Trust and Credibility: _____ 212
Walking the Talk _____ 213
Benefits of Leading with Integrity and Authenticity 215

Challenges of Leading with Integrity and Authenticity: _____ 217
Balancing Personal and Professional Growth _____ 218
Global Leadership Insights _____ 223
Conclusion _____ 225
CHAPTER 10: EXEMPLARY LEADERSHIP _____ 226
My Parents' Example _____ 226
Hardworking and Dedication _____ 228
Honesty and Transparency _____ 229
Responsibility and Accountability _____ 230
Persistence and Resilience _____ 231
Use of Integrity _____ 232
Ethical Decision-Making _____ 233
Building Trust _____ 234
Commitment to Quality: _____ 235
Respect and Fairness _____ 236
Leading With Principles _____ 237
Modeling Desired Behaviors _____ 238
Emotional Intelligence _____ 239
Strategic Thinking _____ 240
Efficiency and Effectiveness _____ 242
Building and Leading Teams _____ 243
Team Dynamics and Collaboration _____ 244
Conflict Resolution _____ 246
Celebrating Success _____ 248
Sustaining Leadership Through Change _____ 249
Global Leadership Insights _____ 250

Conclusion _____ 252
CHAPTER 11: FUTURE GOALS AND ASPIRATIONS 253
    Personal Ambitions _____ 254
    Personal Development _____ 254
    Health and Wellness _____ 255
    Creative Pursuits _____ 257
    Family and Relationships _____ 257
    Community Engagement _____ 259
    Philanthropy and Volunteering _____ 260
    Mentorship and Coaching _____ 261
    Public Speaking and Advocacy _____ 262
    Collaborations with Community Leaders _____ 263
    Global Impact _____ 264
    Global Leadership Insights _____ 266
    Conclusion _____ 267
CHAPTER 12: THE OKUNROUNMU FOUNDATION AND OKUNSGLOBAL ENTERPRISES _____ 269
    The Vision and Mission of Okunrounmu Foundation _____ 269
    Founding Principles: _____ 269
    Core Objectives _____ 270
    Impact and Achievements _____ 271
    Expanding Reach and Scope _____ 271
    Key Initiatives and Projects _____ 272
    The OKUNS GLOBAL Enterprise _____ 274
    Business Ideology _____ 275
    Services and Products _____ 276

Market Expansion — 278
Business Expansion and Innovations — 279
Corporate Social Responsibility (CSR) — 281
Global Leadership Insights — 282
Conclusion — 284
A GLOBAL CALL TO ACTION TO TURN CHALLENGES INTO BOUNDLESS OPPORTUNITIES — 286
YOUR COMMITMENT TO GLOBAL GROWTH AND SUCCESS — 289
MOVING FORWARD WITH YOUR COMMITMENT TO GLOBAL SUCCESS — 291
ABOUT THE AUTHOR — 294

ACKNOWLEDGMENTS

FIRST, I WOULD LIKE TO acknowledge God the Father, the Son, and the Holy Spirit for creating me in His image and giving me dominion over all other things.

My father, Theophilus Akanni, and mother, Beatrice Asabi, have both loved and supported me financially and emotionally throughout my growing years and into adulthood.

I cannot forget my paternal grandmother, Theresa Iyabode, who usually spoiled me with love and gifts during my primary school years; in memory of Sumbo Margaret Okunrounmu, who pushed me out of my comfort zone to leave the shore of Nigeria even before the "Japa" syndrome for my first trip to London.

To my wonderful wife, Oluyemisi Atinuke, who has stuck it out with me since I set my eyes on her in college. I knew that this was my bone of bone and flesh of fresh. She has embodied what true love ♥ is, even when real life is not fun. I love you dearly.

Counting your blessings and naming them individually is to give credit to my children, namely (3Es) Elizabeth, Esther, and Eric, who have been a great source of Joy and inspiration to me.

I cannot forget our grandchildren, AJ, Anjola, and Jordan, our bundles of joy, for all the smiles and fun you give us.

To my brothers and Sisters, I have gained a lot from every one of you.

To all my friends over the decades, I wish to thank you for your roles in my life.

To Mr. Robin Walker, thanks for the IT and technology guide whenever I needed it.

To my manager, Ms. Yolanda Gwathmey, thank you for your undisclosed support, endless supply of strong coffee, and caring smiles.

To all our staff at Okuns Global, Inc. (USA), Okuns Investment Nigeria, Limited, Okunrounmu Foundation Organization, and other vendors named and unnamed for enduring my wavering devotion.

To all the professional colleagues I have worked with over the years, thank you for all the wisdom and knowledge you have shared and received.

To all my spiritual pastors across Continents, I say thank you for your ceaseless prayers.

To Mr. Emmanuel Oso, a great mentor, and for your brother's love for pushing me out of my comfort zone and inspiring me to write this first book.

Lastly, I cannot forget to mention my publishers (Geoffrey Semaganda & wife, Loy), whose presentation at the first meeting was a source of support. Thanks for never giving up on me when I tend to be lazy.

PREFACE

"It's not good enough to want something. It would be best if you planned how to get it," says Dr. Jide Okunrounmu

THIS STATEMENT EMPHASIZES the importance of having a strategy to achieve your goals rather than simply desiring them. Wanting something, whether it is success, happiness, or personal growth, is only the first step. While desire creates motivation, it alone cannot bring about the change or results you seek.

Without a clear plan or actionable steps, those desires remain unfulfilled dreams. Planning structures your ambitions, helping you break big goals into smaller, manageable tasks. It turns abstract wishes into concrete steps that guide you toward your desired outcome. In short, while desire is necessary, planning turns that desire into reality.

In the pursuit of building something significant, one quickly learns that it is not enough to want success. It would be best if you had a plan to achieve it. While desire is a powerful motivator, it must be accompanied by a clear strategy and actionable steps.

This principle is at the core of this book. *Venture Into a Global Entity* is not just about dreaming of global success but about understanding how to grow and scale a venture systematically to reach new heights across borders.

As the title suggests, venturing into a global entity is no small feat. It requires more than ambition; it demands preparation, foresight, and diligent planning. The road to international success is paved with opportunities and challenges requiring thoughtful navigation.

By turning dreams into plans and plans into action, we can transform even the smallest of ventures into thriving global entities. This book is your guide by equipping you with the mindset, tools, and strategies to turn aspirations into tangible achievements on the world stage using my story, life experiences, and lessons learned.

INTRODUCTION

IN A WORLD WHERE challenges often seem impossible, the stories of those who have overcome adversity and carved out paths to success serve as powerful beacons of hope and inspiration. My name is Olajide Okunrounmu (aka Bronco, Jide, Oluyinka, Paul), and my journey from the vibrant streets of Abeokuta, Ogun State, Nigeria, to the bustling cities of London and the expansive landscapes of the United States, is one of the firm foundations of resilience, faith, leadership, and unwavering determination to succeed.

From a young age, I learned the importance of hard work, discipline, and faith. My parents, deeply rooted in their cultural and religious values, instilled in me the significance of education and the power of perseverance. These foundational principles guided me through my formative years and laid the groundwork for my future endeavors.

As an immigrant, I faced numerous challenges, from adapting to new cultures and solid dialects and overcoming systemic obstacles to building a new life from scratch in foreign lands. Yet, through these challenges, I discovered my true strength and potential. My experiences have taught me that adversity is not a barrier but a bridge to success. We can turn our challenges into opportunities through hard work, resilience, and faith.

In this book, *Venture into a Global Entity: Turn Your Adversities into Success Across Continents*, I share my life lessons to empower others. This is not a biography but a guide for those who aspire to rise above their circumstances and achieve greatness wherever they are. I aim to provide insights and lessons that can inspire and guide young people, immigrants, entrepreneurs, parents, and anyone striving to be effective in their lives and the world.

I have always believed in being a pacesetter who forges new paths rather than following the well-trodden ones. This mindset has shaped my approach to life and leadership. I strive to be original, to challenge the status quo, and to inspire others to do the same. My story is a testimony to the power of originality, hard work, and faith in achieving personal and professional fulfillment.

Throughout this book, you will read about my early years in Nigeria, my educational pursuits, and my professional journey across three continents. You will learn about the challenges I faced and the strategies I employed to overcome them. Most importantly, you will see how my faith and commitment to leadership and philanthropy have shaped my life and legacy.

I want to impart the importance of education, hard work, and pursuing one's unique path to youth. To fellow immigrants, I offer my story as a source of strength and a reminder that success is attainable, no matter the obstacles. To all readers, I encourage you to embrace your challenges, stay true to your values, and strive for self-fulfillment.

This book is a call to action to empower humanity, set new standards, and inspire future generations. As you read these pages, I hope you find the motivation to embark on your journey of resilience and global impact. Together, we can create a world where every challenge is an opportunity, and every individual has the potential to be effective.

Let Me Show You How to Turn Your Adversities into Success Across Continents Now!

DR. OLAJIDE OKUNROUNMU

PART 1

AFRICA: MY ROOTS AND FOUNDATIONS

DR. OLAJIDE OKUNROUNMU

CHAPTER 1

SETTING THE STAGE FOR SUCCESS

"SETTING THE STAGE for Success" is more than just a preparatory step; it is the foundation upon which everything else is built. In life, the initial groundwork determines the trajectory of our future. Success is not accidental; it is cultivated through intentional actions, learned resilience, and a clear vision.

This chapter echoes how our early decisions, attitudes, and experiences serve as the critical launchpad for all that follows. By laying a solid foundation, we prepare ourselves to manage the challenges that life inevitably throws at us, ensuring that we have the strength to stay grounded no matter how high we aim.

Empowering Humanity

I was born into the vibrant and culturally rich city of Abeokuta in Ogun State, Nigeria. My early years were a blend of tradition, faith, and ambition. My father, a diligent civil servant, and my mother, a committed petty trader, instilled in me values that have become the cornerstone of my life. From a young age, I was taught the importance of hard work, dedication, and making the most of every opportunity.

As the firstborn, I have always been expected to set a good example for my siblings, guiding them in upholding our family values and dreams. Our forebears laid this foundation by leading through example in our community and church. Growing up, I was often held up as a yardstick for my brothers and sisters, with the weight of responsibility resting on my shoulders. I could not afford to make mistakes, as I was disciplined for my actions and held accountable for my younger siblings' faults. This awareness instilled a deep commitment to our family values, culture, and Christian doctrines, shaping how I have carried myself throughout life.

Being raised in a polygamous household came with its challenges, but my father's commitment to providing for our family never wavered. His decision to invest in property, especially to build a house in Lagos while we lived in a rented apartment, demonstrated his foresight. He taught me that success is not about immediate gratification but laying a foundation for the future. That lesson stayed with me and became a guiding principle as I ventured across continents, pursuing my goals.

Empowering humanity has always been more than my ambition; it has become a calling. I have realized that success is not measured by personal wealth or accolades but by my impact on others. My motivation has always been to become a pacesetter, to lead by example, and to inspire others to rise to their potential.

Whether in my professional life or personal experiences, I've sought to empower those around me, leaving a legacy of strength and inspiration. My father's rise from a simple clerk to a manager at the United Africa Company Nigeria (UACN) left a lasting impression on me. His ability to rise through the ranks was proof that persistence and vision can lead to success.

Overcoming Adversities

The road to success has always been with its challenges. From an early age, I learned that adversity is not a barrier but a tool that strengthens resolve. Growing up in a polygamous family, I witnessed the unique dynamics that come with juggling multiple responsibilities. My father managed it all gracefully, maintaining order and purpose. His discipline, particularly in ensuring that all his children had access to education and resources, left a deep and lasting impression on me.

I was trained to be disciplined and develop a purposeful mindset from childhood. I always strived for the highest in whatever I set my mind to. Education was emphasized during family dinners and prayers and even reinforced through household tasks, making it one of my most powerful tools for overcoming adversity.

My years at St. Benedict's Catholic boarding school were not always easy. Discipline was woven into every aspect of life there, and although I missed my family, the structured environment fostered resilience in me. Waking up early for prayers, completing duties on time, and adhering to strict schedules all helped me develop a sense of responsibility that has guided me throughout my life. That sense of structure became even more critical as I faced future challenges.

My father's job required frequent relocations, so I had to adapt quickly to new environments. This constant change, rather than overwhelming me, taught me the value of adaptability and mental toughness. These qualities became essential when I moved beyond Nigeria to pursue my dreams in the United Kingdom and the United States, as I shared later in the book. Every hurdle I encountered, whether financial, cultural, or professional, became another lesson in resilience, reminding me that success is often born from overcoming difficulties.

Failure is not an option, as my family relies on me for success. My father, who had to abandon his academic pursuits due to financial constraints, vowed that none of his children would face the same hardship. We were taught to face adversity with a learning mindset, constantly asking ourselves what lessons could be gained from challenges. Adversity shaped my path as I progressed through my education and early career.

Global Perspective

I have learned that success is not confined to the immediate surroundings we are born into. This was reflected in the broad mindset instilled by my parents, even when it did not make sense to me at first. I was sent to a Catholic nursery and primary school, where I learned strict Catholic doctrines and mingled with all kinds of people. During my first 25 years, I attended various interstate schools and colleges.

I had the unique opportunity to spend long vacations with my father in different states where he worked. I traveled extensively throughout Nigeria's southern, Christian, and northern, primarily Muslim, regions, allowing me to experience diverse cultures. These experiences prepared me to adapt quickly when I traveled abroad and adjusted to Western cultures. Influenced by its British colonial past, Nigeria's educational system mirrored many aspects of Western culture, further aiding in this transition.

Cultural diversity has been one of the defining aspects of my journey. In London, I was thrust into a world where the cultural norms and societal expectations vastly differed from those I had grown up with in Nigeria. Instead of retreating into my comfort zone, I embraced the differences, learned from the various cultures I encountered, and integrated those lessons into my life. I could navigate life's complexities abroad with greater understanding and grace by valuing those differences.

This openness to cultural diversity continued to shape my life when I moved to the United States. The American Dream, with its promises of prosperity and opportunity, presented its challenges. Yet, I approached those challenges with the resilience I had homed in earlier years. I quickly realized that success in one country might look different from success in another and that achieving it globally required flexibility and understanding of other cultural contexts. This ability to navigate and embrace cultural diversity has been crucial to my personal and professional success.

In my work as an entrepreneur and healthcare professional, having a global perspective has allowed me to build bridges between my Nigerian heritage and the new cultures I have embraced. Success for me is not just about personal achievement; it is about contributing to the communities I find myself in, whether in London, Michigan, or beyond. My story is a testament to the power of embracing the world beyond our immediate surroundings and the endless possibilities when we welcome new experiences with an open heart.

Inspirations and Motivations

Behind every achievement in my life has been a source of inspiration deeply rooted in my upbringing and the people I have encountered. My father, whose work ethic and dedication to our family's well-being inspired me from a young age, was a central figure in shaping who I've become. His unwavering financial and emotional support gave me the foundation to pursue my dreams. But it was not just my family that motivated me; throughout my life, I encountered mentors, colleagues, and even strangers who left lasting impressions on me and pushed me to aim higher.

One such figure was my paternal grandmother, who played a significant role during my time at St. Benedict's Catholic School. Her regular visits, bringing provisions and moral support, were a constant reminder of the importance of family and community. Those small gestures impacted me, reminding me that my roots will always be essential to my journey no matter where life takes me.

As I grew older, my sources of inspiration expanded beyond my family. The broader community of educators, mentors, and professionals I encountered helped shape my worldview. My time in elite schools exposed me to students from diverse backgrounds, further fueling my ambition. Surrounded by peers from wealthy and influential families, I realized that success was not just about hard work but building relationships and networks that could open doors to new opportunities.

My story is filled with these moments of inspiration, whether it was a teacher who simplified a complex subject or a mentor who offered timely advice. Even the challenges I faced in adjusting to life in new countries became sources of motivation, pushing me to strive for excellence and to give back to others through mentorship and philanthropy.

Global Leadership Insights

Perseverance Leads to Growth

Success is not a one-time achievement but a continuous journey. Remaining steadfast helps us face and overcome obstacles.

Lifting Others is Part of the Path

Actual achievement involves personal gains, supporting those around us, and creating a lasting impact for future generations.

Challenges Hold Hidden Advantages

Difficulties should be seen as opportunities to gain experience and develop. Each obstacle is a chance to strengthen our character and skills.

Flexibility Enhances Success

Being open to change and adjusting to new situations is critical in reaching goals, especially in unfamiliar or shifting environments.

Broaden Your Horizons

Expanding your view beyond familiar surroundings can uncover countless opportunities. Welcoming new perspectives and experiences enriches both personal and professional growth.

Conclusion

The foundation we lay in our early years, shaped by our environment, family, and the lessons we learn, sets the course for our future. Every step and every decision becomes a vital thread in the fabric of who we are destined to become. As we have revealed the roots that cultivate success, these experiences are not isolated. They continue to influence the way we approach life's challenges and opportunities.

Moving forward, we will descend into the formative years, showing how family dynamics and early education shaped the values and vision that continue to guide the future. These early influences become the pillars of strength and character that define personal ambitions, leadership, and the ability to rise beyond circumstances.

CHAPTER 2

FORMATIVE YEARS AND INFLUENCES

THE FORMATIVE YEARS are the bedrock upon which an individual's character, values and future ambitions are built. These early experiences, whether within the family or through structured education, often set the course for a person's path in life.

The influence of childhood environments, family dynamics, and the educational system plays a critical role in shaping personality, building resilience, and instilling lifelong values. These early influences help individuals navigate the challenges of adulthood, offering lessons in responsibility, adaptability, and vision that continue to impact their decisions and outlook as they grow.

Family Dynamics

Growing up, I cherished the sense of community in our village. It truly embodied the idea that "it takes a village to raise a child." Everyone knew each other, and there was no room for mischief without consequences. If you misbehaved, you were disciplined, and your parents were promptly informed. There was a deep sense of love, cohesion, and mutual responsibility among the community members. Depending on how one navigates it, this environment could be both a blessing and a challenge.

Initially, our family life was incredibly harmonious. My father, as the sole breadwinner, ensured we never lacked anything. We shared meals, dressed alike, and lived a happy life together. My father did his best to balance his love among his first three wives, creating an atmosphere free of jealousy, insecurity, or neglect. However, this delicate balance unraveled after he married his fourth and fifth wives. This family expansion created strain, and the harmony we once knew faded.

Despite this, there was always strong cohesion among my siblings. We respected each other deeply, and our responsibilities and influence were naturally passed down according to age. My younger siblings often turned to me for advice and direction, and we continued to share meals and daily activities.

Growing up, we were blessed, and our father was considered a successful man who fostered a warm, welcoming environment. Our home became the central gathering place for immediate and extended family, especially during festive periods. We celebrated family values and traditions, including birthdays, Easter, Christmas, New Year, family harvests, and various community celebrations. We also gathered each night to pray together, with our father permanently closing the evening with a blessing.

My father's love for playing the piano meant that many of us became adept at reciting Christian hymns. This shared musical and spiritual connection brought us closer, reinforcing the values of faith, family, and togetherness that shaped our upbringing.

In my family, education was never just an expectation. It was a lifeline. My father's relentless commitment to ensuring that all his children received the best education possible was rooted in his belief that knowledge was the key to escaping limitations.

Attending St. Benedict's Catholic boarding school was one of the first places where I learned the power of structure. Everything about the school was controlled, from waking up early for prayers to adhering to a strict study timetable. Although it was a challenging environment, it fostered in me a discipline that became second nature.

Reading also played a significant role in my personal growth during these years. I devoured novels, biographies, and history books that opened my mind to the world beyond Nigeria. Biographies of influential leaders like Winston Churchill and Nelson Mandela captured my imagination. Their stories of resilience, adaptability, and triumph in adversity inspired me deeply. I began to see how education was more than just a path to academic success; it was the gateway to global opportunities and leadership.

Structured Education and Personal Growth

My formal education began in the structured environment of St. Benedict's Catholic Nursery and Primary School in Abeokuta, Ogun State. The school, run by Catholic missionaries, was known for its discipline and strict routines. I spent six years caring for this educational system, which introduced me to formal learning and instilled in me the value of structure and order. I started with daily morning prayers, emphasizing neatness, punctuality, and diligence.

While the rigid routine was sometimes overwhelming, especially for a young boy, it set the foundation for my academic journey. The emphasis on discipline from such a young age shaped my approach to learning and life, making me realize the importance of time management, responsibility, and hard work.

I had little freedom to socialize outside of school, as the boarding school environment kept us within a strict schedule. Yet, I learned to thrive within those constraints, understanding that the habits formed during those early years would stay with me for life.

Impact of Catholic Disciplines

The influence of the Catholic discipline I received at St. Benedict's was profound. The nuns and priests who ran the school emphasized religious practice and daily prayers were non-negotiable. This routine introduced me to the power of faith and the importance of spiritual grounding, lessons I would carry into adulthood. More than just religion, the school's approach to discipline was integrated into every aspect of our lives. From maintaining clean uniforms to obeying the authority of our teachers, the school drilled a sense of obedience and respect into us.

This environment also left me with a strong sense of order and duty. The school required students to follow strict guidelines, and any deviation from these expectations was met with firm correction. As a result, I learned early on the value of adhering to set rules, a mindset that would become invaluable as I progressed through more advanced academic and professional settings. Looking back, I see how this early exposure to such a disciplined life helped me stay grounded in the face of future challenges.

Community Engagement

Though I spent most of my early years in boarding school, there were opportunities for community engagement that broadened my understanding of the world outside school. During the holidays, I would return home to Lagos, where I could interact more with my local community. However, my engagement with the broader community was limited due to the structured nature of school life. Only during long vacations could I immerse myself in the home environment and engage more with family and neighbors.

During my schooling years, I had few opportunities to participate in community activities through church events and occasional family functions. These experiences helped me understand the importance of social interaction, though my genuine connection to the larger community would not develop fully until my later years in secondary school.

Life in Lagos

Life in Lagos starkly contrasted with the structured world of boarding school. Whenever I returned home for holidays, I was met with the vibrancy and fast pace of the city. Lagos's bustling streets, diverse population, and economic activities opened my eyes to a different side of life.

My mother was actively involved in petty trading, and through her, I witnessed firsthand the challenges and rewards of business life. Watching her work in the marketplaces while managing the household taught me valuable lessons in resilience and adaptability. My father's work as a United Africa Company (UAC) manager also influenced my perception of life in Lagos. Although his career necessitated travel across Nigeria, Lagos was always our home base. His dedication to his work and forward-thinking investment in property left an indelible mark on me. It showed me that even in the demanding environment of Lagos, one could plan carefully and deliberately.

Being in Lagos during the holidays offered a sense of balance to the structured life I led at boarding school. The city's energy and my exposure to various social and economic activities enriched my understanding of life beyond the classroom and helped foster my sense of ambition.

The Power of Education

My middle school years were filled with adventure, growth, and personal discovery. After leaving the confines of primary school, I entered Ayetoro Comprehensive High School in Ogun State, one of Nigeria's most prestigious schools. Moving into this elite institution felt like a new chapter, and I quickly realized that I had to adapt to a new social and academic environment.

The school drew students from various backgrounds, including children of wealthy families, government officials, and middle-class Nigerians like me. The diverse community expanded my worldview and forced me to interact with people from different walks of life.

At Ayetoro, the days were filled with academics and extracurricular activities. I participated actively in the Boy Scouts and inter-house sports competitions, where soccer became one of my favorite pastimes. The structured environment also required us to balance schoolwork with other responsibilities, such as participating in school-organized events and clubs. Despite the challenges, I embraced these experiences, as they helped shape my understanding of teamwork, discipline, and responsibility. The camaraderie among students was strong, and we often leaned on each other for support, whether on the soccer field or in the classroom.

Education transformed my life by moving me from someone who once accepted societal norms without question to a person who actively seeks knowledge and discernment. It has empowered me to identify what is right and wrong, create opportunities for myself, and take decisive action when needed rather than relying on others.

Through education, I have achieved my professional goals and gained financial independence.

Secondary School Life and Lessons

My time at Ayetoro Comprehensive High School was not just about adventure; it was also a period of severe academic growth. As I progressed through the years, I was placed in the science stream, where I found my footing in subjects like biology and agricultural science, even though I faced some difficulties with chemistry. These years were marked by intense competition among students, as Ayetoro was known for producing some of the brightest minds in the country. The school's rigorous academic standards pushed me to strive for excellence constantly.

Life in secondary school was not without its challenges. One of the most difficult aspects was the hierarchy among students, especially the dynamics between senior prefects and junior students. Discipline was often enforced harshly, and as juniors, we were subject to the authority of our seniors.

Although challenging, this experience helped me build resilience and learn how to navigate complex social environments. Despite these challenges, I found solace in my studies and the friendships I built over the years. I also developed a keen interest in debating, where I learned to articulate my thoughts clearly and engage in intellectual discussions with my peers.

One of the defining moments during my secondary school years was when General Olusegun Obasanjo, then the military head of state, visited our school during his tour of Ogun State. His visit left a lasting impression on me. Seeing a leader of such stature visit our school made me realize the importance of leadership and excellence. From that moment, I knew I wanted to grow into a leader who could make a meaningful impact on others, just as General Obasanjo had inspired us. This desire would follow me throughout my life and career.

Initiation Into Leadership Roles

As the firstborn of my parents, I have naturally stepped into leadership roles. This responsibility has shaped me throughout my life, and I have continued to build on it at every stage of my education, from nursery school to college.

Although I had taken on small responsibilities at home, it was not until secondary school that I began to experience the weight of leadership. Midway through my years at Ayetoro, I was given more responsibilities and became involved in student activities that required me to lead and manage groups of my peers.

These leadership roles were often informal, but they helped me realize my ability to organize, motivate, and guide others. I was a part of various student societies and usually found myself at the forefront of initiatives that required coordination and teamwork.

The Boy Scouts played a significant role in my initiation into leadership. I learned important lessons about service, responsibility, and leading by example through scouting activities. As a scout, I participated in community projects that required us to work as a team to achieve common goals. These experiences taught me the importance of collaboration and communication skills that would serve me well professionally and personally in my future leadership roles.

As I approached my final years in secondary school, I became more confident in my leadership abilities. Whether it was leading a school project, organizing events, or mentoring younger students, I embraced these opportunities as steppingstones toward becoming the leader I aspired to be. Each responsibility I took helped refine my ability to manage people, resolve conflicts, and make decisions that benefited the group. This initiation into leadership would continue to shape my future approach to teamwork and leadership.

Lifelong Learning

One of the most significant lessons I learned during my education was the value of lifelong learning. My father always emphasized the importance of education to an end and a continuous process that extends beyond the classroom. His words stayed with me throughout my life, and I began to understand that authentic learning never stops. Even after completing my formal education, I remained curious and open to acquiring new knowledge.

Throughout my academic journey, I was fortunate to have been mentored by several influential teachers who instilled a love for learning. These mentors helped me see the value of continuous improvement and the need to stay intellectually active.

As I moved through secondary school and later into university, this mindset of ongoing education became an integral part of my personal and professional growth. Whether through formal education, professional experiences, or self-guided learning, I am always committed to seeking knowledge, improving my skills, and staying adaptable to change.

This philosophy of lifelong learning shaped my career trajectory as I ventured into healthcare, business, and beyond. I believe that no matter how much one achieves, there is always more to learn, more to explore, and more ways to grow. Learning, after all, is not just about acquiring degrees or certifications; it is about becoming a better version of oneself with every passing day.

Early Lessons of Responsibility

Financial Literacy

I was raised by parents who lived below their means, instilling in me the importance of financial discipline. Thanks to my father's forward-thinking approach to managing our family's resources, I was fortunate to be exposed to financial literacy early.

Although my father was a civil servant, he made decisions that ensured our long-term financial security. One of the most impactful lessons he taught me was the importance of investing in the future. While we lived in a rented apartment in Lagos, my father was already purchasing property, showing me that securing long-term stability was more important than indulging in immediate comforts.

This approach to finance instilled in me the value of saving and investing wisely. I learned that financial stability was not just about earning money but about managing it effectively and making strategic decisions to provide future returns. My father's lessons in financial prudence laid the foundation for my later interest in property investment and entrepreneurship. He demonstrated that our choices today, particularly in economic matters, can have long-lasting impacts on our lives. Watching him manage his resources influenced my outlook on money and taught me how to take calculated risks for future gains.

Accountability

When we were given pocket money for boarding school, we were always required to provide an account of how it was spent. This practice instilled a sense of responsibility and accountability in managing finances from a young age. It taught me the importance of budgeting and being mindful of every expenditure.

Being the eldest son in my family came with a significant amount of responsibility. Even though I was not the firstborn, due to the loss of my parents' first child, I assumed the role of the firstborn. This meant that I was accountable not only to my parents but also to my siblings. The weight of this responsibility was felt from an early age, as I was expected to help guide and take care of my younger brothers and sisters.

My father often traveled due to his work with the United Africa Company (UAC), and during his absence, I usually took over the responsibility of keeping the household in order. Whether ensuring my siblings completed their schoolwork or assisting my mother with household tasks, I learned the importance of accountability early on.

This sense of responsibility extended beyond family duties, as I knew my actions reflected on the family. This early experience with accountability taught me the significance of trust and dependability, qualities that would later be critical in my professional life when leading teams and managing complex projects.

My Catholic upbringing, which emphasized the importance of organization and focus, has taught me valuable lessons in task prioritization. This has helped me develop the ability to prioritize tasks, avoid multitasking, and maintain clarity by planning. I have also learned the significance of setting clear goals, staying focused, establishing boundaries, and understanding when to delegate tasks to ensure everything is managed effectively.

Time Management

Having been trained by Europeans, my dad instilled a strong discipline regarding punctuality in our household; lateness was never tolerated. Every morning, we would wake up early for family prayers, a habit deeply ingrained in me from a young age. This routine continued into my nursery and primary school years when punctuality became second nature.

Time management became a crucial skill for me, particularly as I balanced the demands of school with my responsibilities at home. The structured environment of both St. Benedict's Catholic School and Ayetoro Comprehensive High School required that I adhere to strict schedules. Every aspect of our school day was meticulously planned, from waking up early for prayers to completing our studies in the evening. This routine helped me develop the discipline to manage my time effectively.

However, the need for time management did not end with school. As the eldest son, I was also expected to assist my mother with household chores while keeping up with my studies. Balancing these responsibilities required me to prioritize tasks, ensuring I completed my schoolwork before helping at home.

This early training in time management would become invaluable later in life, especially as I transitioned into higher education and, eventually, my career, where deadlines, multitasking, and managing competing demands became a constant part of my life.

Learning to manage time effectively also helped me develop a sense of personal responsibility. I realized that no matter how many demands were placed on me, I had to organize my time and ensure nothing was neglected. This skill became crucial to my success, enabling me to meet academic and personal obligations without compromising.

Balancing School and Family Expectations

As mentioned, I consistently balanced my academic pursuits from primary education through tertiary college, except for occasional academic disruptions caused by school closures. Family time was cherished during school breaks and holidays, providing an essential opportunity to reconnect and unwind from the demands of education.

Balancing school with family expectations was one of the most challenging aspects of my early years. My parents, especially my father, placed a high value on education, and it was clear that academic success was not optional. It was expected. At the same time, I had a significant role within the family, particularly in helping to care for my younger siblings and supporting my mother in her various business ventures. This balancing act was difficult but necessary, as I was expected to excel in both spheres.

The demands of school were rigorous, particularly during my years at Ayetoro Comprehensive High School, where academic performance was paramount. At home, my father made it clear that my success in school was not just for me but for the family's future. There was an unspoken understanding that I was to set an example for my siblings and that my achievements would pave the way for them to follow.

Managing school and family expectations helped me develop resilience and taught me how to handle pressure. Sometimes, the demands felt overwhelming, but I learned to stay focused and manage my responsibilities in both areas. These early lessons in balancing different aspects of my life prepared me for the challenges I would face later, particularly in balancing the demands of my career with the responsibilities of family life. I understood that balance does not mean perfection; it means ensuring that each part of your life receives the attention it deserves at the right time.

Global Leadership Insights

Long-term Planning is Key to Financial Success

Learning financial literacy early, especially from a role model like my father, taught me the importance of saving and investing for the future. This mindset helped shape my approach to money, emphasizing the need to make calculated decisions prioritizing long-term stability over short-term gratification.

Accountability Builds Trust and Leadership

Being the eldest son taught me that responsibility and accountability are central to becoming a dependable leader. Whether in family life or professional settings, accountability fosters trust and respect, allowing others to rely on your decisions and leadership.

Time Management Enables Success

Managing time effectively became one of my most valuable skills, particularly balancing school and family responsibilities. By prioritizing tasks and developing discipline, I was able to meet the high demands placed on me at a young age. This skill would serve me well throughout my academic and professional career.

Adaptability is Essential for Balancing Multiple Responsibilities

Balancing rigorous academic expectations with family duties helped me build resilience. I learned that life often requires managing competing priorities and adaptability, which is crucial for maintaining balance without compromising essential commitments.

Education is a Lifelong Journey

The power of education goes beyond the classroom. It teaches discipline, responsibility, and resilience. The lessons I learned in middle school and secondary school, as well as from my mentors, highlighted the importance of continual growth and the pursuit of knowledge, setting the foundation for lifelong learning.

Conclusion

We have laid the foundation for understanding how family, culture, and early education shape an individual's values and worldview. These early experiences provide the moral compass and resilience to face future challenges. As we move into higher education and career development, it becomes clear that pursuing knowledge is not just an academic exercise but a transformative journey.

Chapter Three will study how higher education and pursuing a professional career solidify the groundwork for personal and professional success. These years mark a period of intellectual growth, discovery, and the building of expertise, setting the stage for the author's entry into the global workforce and his eventual rise as a leader in his chosen field.

CHAPTER 3

HIGHER EDUCATION AND CAREER DEVELOPMENT

HIGHER EDUCATION PROVIDES individuals with the tools, knowledge, and skills necessary to thrive in a competitive global landscape. It serves as a foundation for career development, offering a space for intellectual exploration, critical thinking, and specialization in various fields. At the same time, career development is a continuous process of setting goals, gaining experience, and refining abilities to succeed in one's chosen profession. These aspects empower individuals to contribute meaningfully to society while pursuing personal fulfillment and long-term achievements.

Polytechnic Years

1982, I sat for my WAEC examination and passed with all my credits. However, my total score did not meet the requirements for my first choice of studying medicine at my preferred universities. As a result, I opted to pursue my (GCE) Advanced Level program at Ogun State Polytechnic. During this time, I lived at my father's house and commuted to college as a day student.

After completing secondary school, I began my journey into higher education at Ogun State Polytechnic. This was a significant shift from the regimented life I had grown accustomed to during my boarding school days. Unlike the highly structured environment of Comprehensive High School, polytechnic life offered a newfound sense of independence. I lived at home during this time, commuting to school daily, which allowed me to balance academic demands with the responsibilities of being the eldest son at home. These two years were a period of intellectual and personal growth, allowing me to explore my interests while preparing me for the next phase of my educational journey.

At the polytechnic, I was exposed to an academic setting emphasizing practical skills and real-world applications. The curriculum was designed to equip students with a strong foundation in their chosen fields, and for me, the focus was on the sciences. This is where my affinity for biology and health-related subjects began to solidify.

However, the pressure to conform to societal expectations remained, as careers in medicine, law, or engineering were considered the pinnacle of success. Despite this, I felt a pull toward a less conventional field of physiotherapy. I began envisioning a career that blended my passion for science with my desire to collaborate closely with people in a healthcare setting.

During my polytechnic years, I also developed a deeper understanding of the importance of financial planning and personal responsibility. Living at home gave me a front-row seat to my father's economic management skills as he continued to invest in property and plan for our future. His strategic approach to saving and investing left a lasting impression on me. I began to see education as more than just an academic pursuit, an investment in my future that would provide me the tools to succeed professionally and financially.

University of Lagos

I studied at Ogun State Polytechnic for two years (1982-1984) before being admitted to the University of Lagos, where I pursued a degree in Physiotherapy.

During that period, parents were accustomed to encouraging their children to pursue prestigious professions like medicine, law, or engineering, the most popular career paths. I initially considered medicine my first career choice but later decided to pursue physiotherapy after seeing a physiotherapist treat an Olympic athlete on television.

This experience sparked my interest in physical medicine, which became my second career choice after medicine. In 1984, I was admitted into the University of Lagos, College of Medicine, located in Idi-Araba, Lagos, for a three-year BSc in Physiotherapy.

Choosing physiotherapy felt like the right decision, as I wanted to focus on physical medicine rather than dealing with blood. Physiotherapy was unknown then, with only three universities in the country offering the course.

Working in physical medicine appealed to me, especially since I was not inclined to deal with blood, a core part of medical practice. Though relatively unknown then, physiotherapy resonated with me, and I decided to follow that path. At the time, only three universities in the country offered it as a course, making it a unique and rare profession.

In 1984, I was admitted to the University of Lagos, College of Medicine at Idi-Araba, Lagos, for a three-year BSc in Physiotherapy. This fulfilled my vision, as I felt more comfortable in physical medicine than dealing with the traditional aspects of medicine.

Life on the university campus was quite a transformation for me. It introduced me to the freedoms and social pressures of student life. Like many students, I became involved in social activism and a vibrant lifestyle. The excitement of Lagos drew me into frequent night parties, socializing with friends, and being in the spotlight. I even became an occasional disco DJ and joined the Hamstring Club, a philanthropic social group, allowing me to navigate the campus social scene easily.

During one of these social outings, I met my future wife, Yemisi Atinuke Ogundola. We encountered each other on a picnic trip to Lekki Beach. She and her sister sat next to me on the bus, and from that moment, I was captivated by her charm and grace. Her humility and quiet strength stood out in a sea of other relationships, and soon enough, she became the most important person in my life.

Academically, my time at university passed quickly. Our class had only nineteen students, and we all completed the program in three years, with most of us graduating with either second-class upper or lower degrees. In 1987, I graduated and was posted to Sokoto in northern Nigeria for my mandatory one-year National Youth Service Corps (NYSC). I was the only Physiotherapist posted to the entire state and was assigned to the Sokoto University Teaching Hospital, where I worked as the sole Physiotherapist.

During my time in Sokoto, I embraced the social life again, often mingling with army personnel and spending many evenings at Mami Market, drinking and enjoying the nightlife. Though the year passed quickly, it was an experience that enriched me both personally and professionally.

After completing my service, I sought employment in the southern part of the country. I was soon hired by the prestigious University of Ife Teaching Hospital (now Obafemi Awolowo Teaching Hospital) in Ile-Ife. However, I was later transferred to another branch hospital at Wesley Hospital in Ilesha, Oyo State, where I worked briefly before deciding to move abroad.

Studying Physiotherapy

The decision to pursue Physiotherapy was not one I took lightly. At the time, it was customary for parents to encourage their children to pursue careers in fields like medicine, law, or engineering positions considered stable and prestigious. While I initially considered a career in medicine, I soon realized that the sight of blood and surgical procedures was not something I could see myself managing every day.

This led me to explore other healthcare options, and during this period of reflection, I discovered physiotherapy. The idea of helping patients recover from physical injuries and improve their quality of life through rehabilitation resonated with me.

What drew me to physiotherapy was its focus on physical medicine rehabilitation, movement, and healing without the invasive aspects of traditional medicine. I was particularly fascinated by the role physiotherapists played in helping athletes recover from injuries. Watching Olympic athletes undergo physiotherapy treatments on television sparked my interest in how the body could be trained to heal through targeted physical therapy. This, combined with my love for biology and anatomy, solidified my decision to pursue a degree in physiotherapy.

The academic program at the University of Lagos was demanding, and our cohort was small, which meant that we received a lot of individualized attention from our professors. We were trained in the technical aspects of physiotherapy, such as manual therapy techniques, therapeutic exercise, electrotherapy, and patient communication and care.

This holistic approach to education made me realize that being a successful physiotherapist required more than technical knowledge; it required empathy, patience, and the ability to motivate patients to participate actively in their recovery.

Academic Achievements

Academically, my time at the University of Lagos was both challenging and rewarding. The intense physiotherapy program required us to balance theoretical coursework with practical, firsthand experience in hospital settings.

One of my academic career highlights was the opportunity to conduct a research project on stroke rehabilitation, a key area in physiotherapy. This project allowed me to explore the intricacies of helping stroke survivors regain mobility and independence, and it gave me a deeper appreciation for the role of physiotherapy in improving patient outcomes.

Throughout my studies, I remained committed to achieving academic excellence. Our cohort was small, with only nineteen students in my class, fostering camaraderie and mutual support. We pushed each other to succeed, and I was proud to graduate in 1987 with a solid academic record.

My degree in physiotherapy marked the culmination of years of hard work and opened the door to a fulfilling career in healthcare, one where I could make a real difference in my patients' lives.

The challenges I faced during my academic journey, from navigating the competitive atmosphere of the University of Lagos to managing the rigorous demands of the physiotherapy program, taught me valuable lessons in resilience, discipline, and the importance of staying focused on my goals. These experiences laid the foundation for my professional success and continue influencing how I approach challenges personally and professionally.

Pro Advancements

Initial Job Experiences

After completing my degree in Physiotherapy at the University of Lagos in 1987, I began my professional journey at Sokoto University Teaching Hospital. This was the first significant step in my career, and it was both an exciting and challenging transition from student life to professional practice. Sokoto, located in the northern region of Nigeria, vastly differed from the bustling urban environment of Lagos, where I had spent most of my life. Working in this environment offered me invaluable lessons about the healthcare system and the complexities of patient care, especially in a region where resources were limited and traditional medical practices were still prevalent.

My first role as a physiotherapist was in a hospital setting, where I treated patients suffering from a range of conditions, including musculoskeletal injuries and chronic illnesses. This experience allowed me to apply the skills I had learned during my academic training. Still, it also exposed me to the reality of working in a region with underdeveloped healthcare infrastructure.

The challenges of working in Sokoto extended beyond the clinical setting. The hospital was often overcrowded, and we had to work with limited equipment, making it necessary to improvise and adapt our treatments to fit the resources available. This experience shaped my understanding of providing adequate care, even under challenging circumstances.

National Youth Service

As part of Nigeria's mandatory National Youth Service Corps (NYSC), I was posted to Sokoto for my one-year service. The NYSC program was designed to promote national unity and foster development by sending graduates to regions outside their home states. This was an opportunity to serve my country and gain practical experience in physiotherapy. Working at Sokoto University Teaching Hospital during this time was a pivotal moment in my career and a period of personal growth.

One of the most unforgettable experiences during my NYSC year came early in my service. I was settling into my role at the hospital when I encountered a severely malnourished child who was brought in for therapy evaluation. The child, though nine years old, appeared to be no older than two due to the extent of her malnutrition.

I was exhausted from the morning's workload and was eager to head to lunch, so without thoroughly assessing her condition, I sent the child back to the ward, deeming her too weak for exercise. It was only later that I learned she had died in transit between our rehabilitation gymnasium and the ward.

The news was a jolt to my system, a stark reminder that our decisions as healthcare professionals can have life-or-death consequences. That moment has stayed with me ever since, shaping how I approach patient care and reminding me of the gravity of my chosen profession.

In Sokoto, the realities of practicing in a healthcare system with limited resources and high patient demand became apparent. Unlike the structured and resource-abundant environment I had experienced during my university days, this was a place where I had to rely on my instincts, adaptability, and creative problem-solving to make a difference.

Experiences in the Northern Region

Practicing in the northern region of Nigeria presented a unique set of challenges and opportunities for growth. Sokoto, a Fulani/Hausa area, vastly differed from the southern part of the country where I had grown up and trained. The cultural and religious practices in the region often clashed with modern medical approaches, and as healthcare providers, we were constantly navigating these differences.

Many patients relied on traditional healing methods or herbal remedies, often seeking medical care only when those options failed. Therefore, we needed to provide treatment and educate the patients and their families on the benefits of modern medicine.

The northern region was also plagued by a high rate of disabilities, many of which were preventable or treatable. The lack of access to proper healthcare services and the widespread ignorance of medical practices meant that we were dealing with advanced cases of musculoskeletal disorders, infections, and other chronic conditions that had been left untreated for long periods.

One of the most common challenges was the local population's resistance to seeking hospital care, as many people preferred traditional or religious healing methods. This resistance was often rooted in deep-seated cultural beliefs, and our job was to bridge that gap through education and patient engagement.

Working in Sokoto taught me the importance of healthcare education. We spent significant time treating patients and educating them on basic hygiene, nutrition, and the benefits of early medical intervention.

This was particularly important in a region where healthcare resources were scarce, and proper education could have prevented many illnesses. During this period, I realized the profound impact that healthcare education could have on improving the overall well-being of a community.

Building Resilience

I have used adaptability to bounce back from near-life-threatening adversity, challenges, or stressful situations to advance my personal and professional goals.

Parents' Voices and Wisdom

The wisdom of my parents has been a guiding force throughout my life. My mother's journey through childbirth was marked by immense hardship. She experienced three miscarriages early on, and this became one of the reasons my father chose to marry additional wives, seeking to build a large family in line with his traditional beliefs.

My father, whose own mother had suffered similar miscarriages, bore the middle name Akanni, meaning "warrior child," a reflection of the resilience passed down through generations. These experiences profoundly influenced how my parents' approached life, family, and their children's future.

Growing up, I was constantly surrounded by my parents' voices of wisdom. They wanted the best for me, and their constructive guidance shaped how I saw the world. My father emphasized the importance of hard work, foresight, and responsibility, which would become the cornerstone of my approach to life.

My mother's resilience, seen through her ability to rise above personal loss, inspired me to stay strong despite adversity. Together, their words were like a compass, always pointing me toward the right path. No matter what obstacles I encountered, their advice became my anchor, guiding me toward personal and professional success.

Adapting to Change

Change has always been a constant in my life, and I learned early on that adapting to change is not just about surviving; it is about thriving. I often think of the airplane oxygen mask metaphor: you must secure your mask before helping others. This metaphor has been a powerful reminder that I cannot be a blessing to others without first ensuring that I am in a strong position.

I have learned that life's challenges and obstacles are not barriers to success but bridges. Each setback provides an opportunity to gain experience, and I've always made it a point to learn from those around me who are more experienced and knowledgeable.

I have adapted to change throughout my life by surrounding myself with people who are better than me in various areas. I have refined my path by observing and learning from their successes and failures. I have never let my ego get in the way of my growth, knowing that the most significant lessons come from those who have walked the path before me.

As the saying goes, "Iron sharpens iron," I have applied this principle in my personal and professional development. My habit of reading extensively from a young age also helped me build the flexibility needed to adapt to life's changes. Readers, after all, are leaders, and through books, I have gained the knowledge and insights that have shaped my ability to embrace change and use it to my advantage.

Facing Failure

I have encountered failure at various points but never allowed it to define me. Instead, I have always approached failure as a learning tool, a step toward growth. I have four fundamental principles when handling failure: I can either advertise it, minimize it, maximize it, or learn from it.

My approach has always focused on the lessons that failure can teach. I have never allowed low self-esteem or negative thoughts to cloud my judgment. Instead, I have developed a positive, growth-oriented mindset that helps me view failure as a temporary setback rather than a permanent state.

Whenever I have faced failure, I have taken the time to reflect on what went wrong and how I could have done things differently. This process of self-reflection has been crucial in helping me move forward with a clearer understanding of what needs to change.

I have always craved a growth mindset amid challenges, believing every failure brings the opportunity to gain experience and something valuable. By embracing failure and using it as a tool for growth, I have navigated life's ups and downs with a sense of resilience and optimism.

Developing Mental Toughness

Being born into a large, polygamous family as the firstborn came with a unique set of challenges that helped me develop mental toughness from an early age. Growing up, I had to learn how to navigate the complex dynamics of a large family while also shouldering the responsibilities of being the eldest child. These experiences taught me the importance of self-awareness.

Over the years, I have consistently applied the SWOT analysis (Strengths, Weaknesses, Opportunities, and Threats) to understand better my strengths, weaknesses, and emotional triggers. This process of self-reflection has been instrumental in helping me identify areas where I need to improve, both personally and professionally.

To build mental toughness, I have always made it a point to bounce back from setbacks with a renewed focus and determination. I have developed resilience through consistent self-improvement and spent countless hours reading self-development books on building personal capacity and mental strength. One of the critical lessons I have learned is that decision-making is a skill that requires constant practice.

Over the years, I have learned the importance of seeking wisdom from other elders, colleagues, or family members when making important decisions. This approach has allowed me to develop a more nuanced understanding of my challenges and has helped me grow as a person and a leader.

Overcoming Adversities as Preparation

Childhood Challenges

Growing up in a large polygamous family came with its own set of unique challenges. As a child, I often found myself unable to voice my opinions regarding decisions about my health. My father, deeply rooted in traditional beliefs, had a strong inclination toward using traditional medicine alongside modern medicine. I struggled with this significantly as I grew older and developed my perspectives on healthcare.

Despite my reservations, as a child, I could not challenge the choices made for me, which left me feeling powerless in many instances. It was not until I matured that I felt confident enough to oppose certain traditional practices, particularly those that conflicted with my understanding of modern medicine.

Another significant challenge I faced was the early separation from my parents. Frequent transitions from one household to another were common, as my father's work took him across different regions of Nigeria. This constant movement and the large family structure made it difficult to form stable emotional bonds with my parents and siblings.

At times, I longed for the freedom to escape from the strict upbringing and the complexities of being part of such a large family. There were moments when I felt insecure about our family dynamics, particularly how others perceived our polygamous setup. As a child, I often wished for a simpler, more conventional family life where the burdens of large-scale familial obligations were less prominent.

Despite these challenges, they played an essential role in shaping my resilience. The feelings of insecurity and separation, while challenging to navigate at the time, taught me to be adaptable and self-reliant. They prepared me for the transitions and challenges I would face later in life, especially as I moved from one stage of education to the next and eventually into my career.

Financial Challenges

When it came to financial matters, I was fortunate not to experience significant struggles, thanks to my father's trust in my ability to handle money. From a young age, I was responsible for my finances, with my father opening a bank account for me as soon as I entered Polytechnic College. This early empowerment gave me a sense of independence and financial freedom many of my peers did not have.

However, with that freedom came the responsibility of justifying how I spent the money. My father was keen on teaching me the value of financial prudence. I learned quickly that managing money wisely was about meeting my needs and making strategic choices that would benefit me in the long run.

When I transitioned to university, this financial independence continued to grow. Having access to money during my university years allowed me to make decisions about my life without constantly seeking approval from my parents. It allowed me to explore different avenues of personal growth and pursue what made me happy.

This financial empowerment also enabled me to help others. Throughout high school and college, I was known among my peers for my willingness to share my resources and lend a helping hand when needed. I believe this freedom in financial matters contributed significantly to my self-reliance and confidence to make bold choices in my personal and professional life.

While financially stable during my youth, I always remembered my father's lessons, making prudent decisions and ensuring that I did not take my financial freedom for granted. These lessons would later become vital as I ventured into business and investment, using the economic principles I learned during these early years to make sound investments and grow my wealth responsibly.

Higher Education Aspirations

From an early age, I knew that education would be the key to unlocking opportunities in life. It was not just about getting a degree; higher education was about expanding my horizons, enhancing my critical thinking skills, and positioning myself for success in the global labor market. I always aspired to reach the pinnacle of my profession, which meant pursuing a degree and a doctorate in my chosen field. Throughout my career, I sought opportunities to learn and grow, seizing every chance to attend seminars, join professional bodies, and contribute to academic research.

I became a member of several prestigious organizations, including the Nigeria Society of Physiotherapy, the Council of Allied Supplementary to Medicine in the UK, and the American Physical Therapy Association (APTA). These organizations helped me stay connected to advancements in my field and allowed me to expand my network of professionals worldwide.

My commitment to lifelong learning culminated in 2014, when I earned my doctorate in Physiotherapy from Utica College, New York. Achieving this milestone was one of my life's proudest moments, representing years of dedication, perseverance, and a desire to excel in my field.

Pursuing higher education was about personal achievement and contributing to the broader field of physiotherapy. I have always believed that enhancing my knowledge and skills could better serve my patients and the communities I work with. Completing my doctorate with a high GPA was a testament to my hard work and the belief that education is a lifelong journey that should never be limited by age or circumstance.

Setting Personal Goals

Throughout my life, I have always been focused on setting and achieving goals that align with my personal and professional aspirations. One of the most valuable lessons I learned during my postgraduate studies was the importance of setting SMART goals: Specific, Measurable, Attainable, Relevant, and Time-bound goals. I applied this approach to my academic pursuits, business ventures, and philanthropic efforts. Whether working on a real estate investment or planning a new business venture, I ensured that each goal I set was aligned with these principles.

For me, success is not just about personal achievement. It is about making a lasting impact on others. I have always envisioned building a global brand that would allow me to touch the lives of the less privileged in my community and beyond. This desire to give back has driven many of my business decisions, from investing in real estate and stocks to creating business ventures, allowing me to support charitable causes.

I aim to build a legacy through my work with Okuns Brand, a consultancy, rental, rehabilitation, and foundation enterprise. I envision this brand becoming a global entity that generates wealth and creates opportunities for the less fortunate.

As I continue to set personal goals, I am committed to achieving them before I reach sixty. Whether through philanthropy, business, or personal growth, I am focused on making a meaningful impact in everything I do. Success is measured by what we achieve for ourselves and what we give back to others.

Global Leadership Insights

Resilience is Forged Through Early Challenges

The challenges we face in childhood, whether familial, cultural, or personal, shape our ability to adapt and thrive in adulthood. Overcoming early insecurities and navigating complex family dynamics taught me the value of adaptability and self-reliance, critical traits for leadership in a global context.

Financial Independence Fuels Growth

Gaining financial responsibility at an early age provides the foundation for self-confidence and decision-making. Learning to handle money wisely and independently empowers personal freedom and prepares future leaders to make thoughtful, impactful financial decisions for themselves and those they lead.

Higher Education Opens Global Opportunities

Education is more than just a degree; it is a lifelong pursuit that continually broadens our horizons. By seeking out opportunities for advanced learning, joining professional networks, and contributing to my field, I positioned myself for global success. I ensured that my impact extended beyond my immediate environment.

Set Ambitious, Purpose-Driven Goals

Setting Specific, Measurable, Attainable, Relevant, and Time-bound (SMART) goals helps transform ambition into reality. Through a clear vision for both personal achievement and global impact, leaders can create lasting legacies that inspire and empower others, leaving a positive imprint on their communities and the world.

Failure is a Boulder to Success

Every failure is an opportunity to learn, reflect, and grow. By embracing failure as part of the leadership journey and using it as a tool for continuous improvement, we develop the mental toughness necessary to navigate the complexities of leadership in an ever-changing world.

Conclusion

The roots of my journey are firmly planted in the rich soil of Africa, where the values of resilience, purpose, and perseverance were cultivated. These foundational years, filled with challenges and growth, have shaped my character and prepared me to step onto a larger stage. Every lesson learned, and every struggle overcome has become a source of strength, guiding me toward an evolving vision beyond borders.

As I leave the familiar grounds of my beginnings, I prepare to embrace a future where new barriers will test my resolve and offer greater possibilities. In Part Two ahead, we enter uncharted territory where the drive to succeed meets the unknown and where the influence of my roots will collide with a world that demands even more of me.

PART 2

EUROPE: CROSSING BORDERS AND BREAKING BARRIERS

DR. OLAJIDE OKUNROUNMU

CHAPTER 4

NEW BEGINNINGS IN LONDON

NEW BEGINNINGS SYMBOLIZE fresh opportunities and the chance to embrace change, whether in personal or professional aspects of life. They often come with excitement and uncertainty, but they allow redefining goals, learning from past experiences, and stepping into uncharted territory with renewed energy.

They promise transformation, whether prompted by life transitions, career shifts, or personal growth. They allow individuals to take control of their future, pursue new dreams, and build a stronger, more fulfilling path forward. Each new start presents a moment to realign priorities and create lasting impacts.

Stepping Into the Unknown

Stepping into the unknown is often an inevitable part of personal growth and success. It is the moment when we decide to leave behind the comfort of the familiar and venture into uncharted territory, not knowing what lies ahead but trusting in our ability to adapt and persevere.

Pursuing a new career path, moving to a different country, or taking on new responsibilities, these experiences test our resilience, courage, and determination. While the unknown can bring uncertainty, it also opens doors to new opportunities and discoveries that can shape our future in ways we never imagined.

The Motivation Behind Migration

Leaving Nigeria for London in 1988 was not a decision I made lightly. My life in Nigeria was defined by its limitations working at Obafemi Awolowo Teaching Hospital and Wesley Hospital, where I earned a modest salary as a grade 8 level 2 staff member. Despite my professional training, the financial rewards were minimal. Every month, my salary seemed to vanish as soon as it arrived, consumed by my social lifestyle and daily expenses.

I realized that staying in Nigeria would only prolong my financial struggles. The allure of working abroad, where I could earn more and have better growth opportunities, became impossible to ignore. Many Nigerians left the country, chasing the proverbial "golden opportunity." This was not just about seeking higher pay but fulfilling a larger vision of becoming a global entity in my field.

Beyond the personal financial limitations, there were deeper national issues at play that pushed me to leave. Nigeria's economy was in decline, with inflation rising, healthcare services deteriorating, and educational institutions crumbling. Graduates were leaving universities only to face unemployment, and the public healthcare system was in shambles.

Hospitals lacked the essential drugs, water, and equipment for adequate care. There was little hope that things would improve, as the country's leadership was marked by corruption, waste, and indiscipline. Watching my homeland fall into disarray made it clear that I needed to leave if I wanted to improve my life and prospects.

While my parents did not question my decision to move abroad, they were unaware of the steps I took to obtain my visa. With the help of my uncle's wife, Margaret Sumbo, I navigated the complex visa process and secured a visiting visa. Although I told my parents and others it was a temporary trip, my intention was clear: I would not return until I had established a stable career and life in London.

The real motivation behind this move was not just the pursuit of a better life but a desire to improve myself, acquire more knowledge, and escape the stagnation that had overtaken Nigeria. With dreams of a better future and faith that my persistence would pay off, I stepped onto the plane to London, determined to overcome whatever obstacles lay ahead.

First Impressions and Initial Obstacles

Arriving in London felt surreal, but the reality of my situation set in almost immediately. I had entered a city, unlike the romanticized version I had imagined. The weather alone was a shock. London's cold, especially during the fall and winter, was unlike anything I had ever experienced.

Coming from the warmth of Nigeria, I was ill-prepared for the biting cold that greeted me upon arrival. It was hard to fathom why I had left a warm, comfortable climate only to find myself shivering in a foreign city under the pretense of a vacation.

In addition to the climate shock, I quickly realized that my visa situation was not what I had hoped. The visiting visa I had obtained did not permit me to work legally, which added a new layer of complexity to my plans. This was a blow I had not anticipated, forcing me to reconsider my entire strategy for survival in this new environment.

With no legal means of earning an income, I had to find odd jobs to make ends meet. I took on under-the-table work, anything that would keep me afloat, but nothing was stable or aligned with my professional aspirations. My cousin, Joyce Adeyemo, kindly let me stay with her and her fiancé, but their small room was already cramped, and I knew I could not impose on them for long.

I wandered the streets of London, going from one job agency to another, hoping to find something more stable, but I was repeatedly turned away. My confidence in my qualifications began to wane as I faced the stark reality of my situation. I was an outsider in a foreign land, stuck in legal limbo, unable to work the jobs I had trained for.

It was not just the visa restrictions that caused the cultural shock. Everything felt foreign, from the accents to the way people interacted. I quickly learned that finding a job, let alone one in my field, would not be as easy as I had hoped.

Despite the obstacles, I knew I could not give up. Every rejection pushed me to rethink my strategy. I was determined to make a life for myself here, but it became clear that the journey would require far more resilience and adaptation than I had imagined.

From Financial Abundance to Struggles

Leaving the comfort of Nigeria, where my parents often assisted with any financial shortfalls, to land in London was a stark contrast to the life I had known. Although my salary was low at home, I could always count on my parents' support when things became tight. The support I had in Nigeria was comforting, and despite the limitations of my earnings, I never felt like I was indeed on my own.

However, when I arrived in London, I quickly realized this safety net no longer existed. I had stepped into a completely different reality, where I had no one to fall back on financially, and every decision I made was now critical to my survival.

London, far from being the land paved with gold many had romanticized, was full of people barely scraping by. Everyone I encountered seemed to be living from paycheck to paycheck, struggling to make ends meet. The misconception back home that moving abroad would bring instant prosperity was quickly shattered.

I found myself surrounded by people juggling multiple jobs to stay afloat, and it became apparent that the struggle for survival in London was no less than what I had experienced in Nigeria. If anything, it was more intense. Without the support of my family or any significant savings, I realized that I had to make drastic adjustments to my expectations and lifestyle.

However limited, my financial freedom in Nigeria had given me room to focus on my personal growth and enjoy certain comforts. In London, those comforts were stripped away, and the harsh reality of survival hit me. I no longer had the security of a steady job in my professional field, nor could I count on occasional financial assistance from family.

It was now up to me to find ways to support myself, even if that meant taking on jobs far beneath my qualifications. I quickly learned that in London, even highly educated and skilled workers could be overqualified for the jobs they were forced to take to keep a roof over their heads. This humbling experience redefined my understanding of financial struggle, pushing me to adapt and find new ways to sustain myself.

Job Hunting and Hopping

In my early days in London, finding stable work was almost impossible. With no legal work visa and few connections, I shuttled between different under-the-table jobs to keep body and soul together. These jobs were far from my envisioned professional career but necessary for survival.

I had to devise creative "strategies to survive" in a city that did not seem to care about my qualifications or ambitions. The work I took on was about survival, not fulfillment, and often, it barely covered my rent, which had to be paid weekly or monthly from the meager income I scraped together.

I bounced from one job to another, taking on whatever was available. I was a Subway cook, flipping sandwiches in a fast-paced, chaotic environment. The pay was low, and the hours were long, but it was something I could hold onto for the time being.

I also tried my hand as a sales agent, attempting to sell products door-to-door. That was short-lived, as it barely dented my financial needs. On top of these jobs, I worked as an in-house cleaner, scrubbing floors and cleaning office buildings in the early hours of the morning before anyone arrived for the day.

As a postmaster, one of my toughest jobs was delivering mail in London's chilling winter weather. No transportation options were provided, so I had to carry heavy mail bags while trekking through the streets on foot. The cold was unlike anything I had ever experienced, biting through my bones as I struggled to keep up with the job demands.

Then came my short-lived stint as a bricklayer, a job for which I had no training or physical stamina. The work was grueling, and after a single day on site, the foreman took one look at my hands, soft and unaccustomed to manual labor, and told me not to come back the next day.

Each job pushed me through the fire and onto the frying pan of life as an immigrant worker. The work was exhausting, the pay was poor, and the constant instability weighed heavily on me. But each role taught me about survival, resilience, and the strength to endure adversity.

I learned to adapt, to take whatever was available, and to do what was necessary to survive. It was a humbling experience, and while it was not the path I had envisioned, it would build the fortitude I needed to succeed in the long run.

Embracing Change

The Emotional Landscape

Upon arriving in London, the first significant challenge was physical and emotional. The shift from the warmth of Nigeria to the chilling cold of London's fall and winter months was harsh. Beyond the weather, the profound realization hit that wealth was not equitably distributed, even in a developed nation like the United Kingdom.

It was clear that despite the allure of foreign lands, immigrants had to navigate a complex social class system that could be just as stifling as back home. I understood firsthand that a country's wealth does not necessarily translate to the well-being of its people and that prospective immigrants are often unaware of this misconception.

These early realizations about the layers of British society were eye-opening. The immense wealth associated with the British aristocracy contrasted starkly with the everyday struggles of many citizens and immigrants. This emotional journey helped to reshape my perspective about life abroad. It became evident that prosperity was not guaranteed simply by crossing borders and that systemic challenges existed even in so-called advanced nations.

Adapting to British Culture

Adapting to British culture required significant adjustments, not just in how I communicated but also in how I viewed and interacted with the world around me. British society is deeply rooted in respect and etiquette behaviors that starkly differ from Nigeria's chaotic and sometimes aggressive lifestyle. Here, politeness and queuing were not merely courtesies but essential aspects of life. I had to embrace this system, learning to patiently wait my turn, to say "please" and "thank you," and to navigate the unspoken social rules that seemed embedded in everyday interactions.

Tea drinking, for example, was not just a simple beverage but a symbol of British social interaction. Offering tea and biscuits became a way to demonstrate hospitality and engage in conversations. Unlike in Nigeria, where one might push through a crowded room or rely on social status to get ahead, British society taught me the value of waiting, humility, and outward respect for others. These cultural nuances were critical in helping me establish personal and professional relationships, and learning them became an integral part of my growth.

Maintaining Nigerian Identity

Despite the need to adapt, I found it essential to maintain my Nigerian identity. My accent, cultural attire, and connection to the Nigerian community in London helped keep me grounded. As much as I had to integrate into British society, I refused to let go of my heritage. I was determined to stay true to myself, to preserve my roots, and to carry forward the traditions that defined me.

Within the Nigerian immigrant community, we maintained a sense of home. We spoke our local dialects, greeted each other with traditional greetings, and often gathered in places that reminded us of Nigeria. Shopping at places like Liverpool Market became a hub for connecting with familiar faces and finding the foods and items that kept our culture alive. Our churches, too, became sanctuaries for preserving our faith and customs, offering a much-needed reprieve from the daily grind of life abroad.

Breaking Professional Barriers

Breaking into the professional world was no easy feat. The lengthy process of getting my Nigerian qualifications recognized by British authorities was a significant obstacle. It took several months before my degree from the University of Lagos was accepted by the professional body in London. The sting of realizing that other African degrees were not held in equal regard to those from Western institutions was another reminder of the disparities that existed for immigrants.

Nevertheless, I was determined to practice physiotherapy in the UK. Once I had cleared the certification hurdles, I joined a recruitment agency that placed me in hospitals across London and Southeast England. The exposure I gained was invaluable. I worked in state-of-the-art hospitals with access to equipment and techniques I had only read about during my undergraduate years in Nigeria.

The hands-on approach in the UK allowed me to hone my skills further and prepared me for future endeavors in the United States. However, these opportunities did not come quickly, and I had to juggle several odd jobs before securing a stable professional role. Yet, this experience taught me persistence and adaptability, crucial to thriving in foreign environments.

Marriage and Starting a Family

Saying I Do

Saying "I do" is never a simple decision, but it became necessary in London. My fiancée, Oluyemisi, and I had been planning a future together for a while. Although we had already introduced each other to our respective families back in Nigeria, circumstances in London hastened the formalization of our relationship.

Five months after my arrival, I realized marriage was not just about love and commitment. It was a strategy for survival. The uncertainty of my immigration status weighed heavily on me. I knew that by marrying a British citizen, I could secure my stay in the UK without the constant fear of deportation or the endless cycle of visa renewals.

On the day of our wedding, we kept things simple. We headed to the courthouse with a small group: Oluyemisi, myself, my Uncle Wale (who doubled as our photographer), and a visiting friend, Mrs. Abereoje. We were married in August 1989 in a quiet, understated ceremony, a far cry from the elaborate weddings I had imagined back in Nigeria. Still, it was a breath of fresh air for both of us. Despite the low-key nature of our wedding, the relief I felt was immense. This marriage opened the door to a more secure future for myself and the life Oluyemisi and I were building together.

Even though we did not inform our families back in Nigeria about the courthouse wedding at the time, we knew that as the firstborn in our respective families and with our deep Christian faith, a proper church wedding was inevitable.

The unspoken expectation from both sides of the family meant that a grander celebration was necessary. So, we began to plan our church wedding, setting a date for July 7th, 1990, a day that would bring together our families from Nigeria and Japan to witness the union they had long anticipated.

Balance Work and Home Life

In the months leading up to our church wedding, life became a whirlwind of activity. Oluyemisi and I were determined to save as much money as possible to fund the wedding and secure our future. My wife worked as an auxiliary nurse while still pursuing her full certification, while I juggled multiple jobs to make ends meet.

My main job was as a full-fledged physiotherapist, working the standard eight-hour shifts from 8 a.m. to 4 p.m. But that was not enough. To boost our income, I took on a permanent evening cleaning job from 5 p.m. to 7 p.m., scrubbing offices and warehouses.

The real challenge came with my night shift at the Coca-Cola warehouse, where I worked from 10 p.m. to 6 a.m., sorting bottles and packaging products. This grueling job left me physically and mentally exhausted, as I struggled to stay awake throughout the night.

I often slept through the shifts, but I knew I had no choice but to push through. The weight of responsibility was heavy, and I had to provide for my wife and prepare for the next stage of our lives.

During this time, we moved twice within North London, trying to balance affordability and convenience. The pressure of working multiple jobs while managing a home life was intense, but I knew it was temporary. We were both in a race against time, with the wedding approaching and financial obligations piling up. Then, amid all this chaos, my wife revealed that she was pregnant. The news hit me like a tidal wave: how would we manage a pregnancy on top of everything else? But, as with everything else in life, I accepted the challenge head-on.

The Quest for Health Solutions

Pregnancy brought a new layer of complexity to our already busy lives. Oluyemisi had been diagnosed with Type 1 diabetes during her undergraduate years at Lagos University Teaching Hospital (LUTH), and her health required careful monitoring. The pregnancy intensified her condition, and her work schedule had to be drastically reduced to accommodate frequent doctor visits and health checks. The worry weighed heavily on both of us, especially with the wedding approaching.

An unexpected opportunity came knocking as I struggled to balance work and home life. During my early days in London, I had applied for jobs in the United States, but I had not expected much to come from it. However, as fate would have it, I received a job offer from a hospital in the U.S., and to my surprise, they sent two representatives to London to interview me in person.

The offer was beautiful: higher pay, better benefits, and the promise of a more stable life. It was hard to believe that after all the struggles in London, the door to America was opening. But this presented a new dilemma. We were already settled in London, with income streams, and now a baby on the way. Moving across the Atlantic would complicate things even further. Yet, the opportunity was too good to pass up. I accepted the job offer, knowing that this would take our family into a new chapter.

Our First Bundle of Joy

Despite all the challenges we faced in the months leading up to the wedding, July 7th, 1990, turned out to be a glorious day. We were married in a beautiful church ceremony at the Methodist Church in Finsbury, London, surrounded by family and friends from all over.

Our parents, who had initially been unaware of our courthouse wedding, finally had the chance to witness our union in a formal setting with all the grandeur they had expected. It was a day filled with joy, laughter, and celebration, marking the beginning of our next chapter as husband and wife.

Just a month later, our daughter, Elizabeth Moronke Okunrounmu, was born on August 19th, 1990, at Middlesex

Hospital in London. She was our first child, our princess, and the embodiment of our hopes and dreams. However, the joy of her birth was bittersweet for me. Just nine days before her arrival, I had left London to begin my new job in the United States. Leaving my wife behind, heavily pregnant, was one of the most complex decisions I had to make, but I knew that securing our future in America was essential for our family's growth.

The birth of Elizabeth marked the beginning of a new chapter filled with even more significant challenges and adventures. Our lives were about to take a dramatic turn as we embarked on this new journey, moving from London to the United States. The experiences we had gained in London, both the triumphs and the struggles, had prepared us for what lay ahead. But little did we know that the adventure was only beginning.

Preparing for Another Transition

The Blessed Opportunity

Just as I started to find my rhythm in London after navigating numerous challenges and setbacks, a new door of opportunity swung open. I had overcome the initial cultural shock, secured a stable job, and found comfort in the life my wife and I were building. But then came an unexpected blessing: an offer of a job in the United States. The U.S. had always represented the ultimate destination, the land of opportunity where success and freedom awaited those willing to work for it. For many, it was "God's own country," and now, I had the chance to be part of that dream.

It was an incredible blessing, but the timing was bittersweet. My wife was in the third trimester of her pregnancy with our first child, and the thought of leaving her behind while I started a new life in America filled me with mixed emotions. On the one hand, I knew this was a once-in-a-lifetime opportunity that could change our lives' trajectory. On the other hand, it was difficult to leave my wife at such a critical moment in our family's journey. Yet, when God opens the window of heaven, you must receive the blessing with thanksgiving. I knew this opportunity had to be seized despite the personal challenges it presented.

Visa and Immigration Process

The visa and immigration process for moving from the UK to the United States was far less complicated than I had anticipated. My marriage to a British citizen had already secured me temporary permanent residency in the UK, which made the transition smoother. The job offer I received in the U.S. came with full support from my new employer, who handled all the H-1 visa paperwork on my behalf. This transition was seamless, unlike the painstaking process of securing my physiotherapy license in the UK.

VENTURE INTO A GLOBAL ENTITY

On August 10th, 1990, I boarded a flight bound for the United States, leaving behind a pregnant wife and the familiarity of London. Nine days later, on August 19th, 1990, our daughter was born in London; it was a bittersweet moment for me as I was across the Atlantic, starting a new phase while missing one of the most significant moments in our lives.

Although challenging, I knew this move was necessary for our family's future. The ease of the immigration process was a relief, but the emotional weight of leaving my wife and newborn daughter behind was a burden I carried with me as I stepped onto American soil.

Professional Integration

Arriving in the U.S. was a cultural shock. Unlike the formal British workplace, where I had spent the last few years in suits and ties, I was greeted at Detroit Metropolitan Airport by two more laid-back colleagues. There I stood, sweating in my formal British suit, expecting a similar professional environment, only to realize that Americans had a far more relaxed approach to work attire and lifestyle. It was a stark reminder that I was entering a new world where I needed to adapt quickly.

However, unlike my experience in London, where I had to start from scratch, the transition into my new professional role in the U.S. was much smoother. My employer had processed my visa and arranged housing for me. After spending just three days in a hotel, I moved into a two-bedroom apartment. This immediate support made all the difference in easing the transition. While different from the UK's, the American healthcare system was a new frontier for me, and I was eager to integrate into it.

The equipment and techniques used in physiotherapy in the U.S. were far more advanced than those in the UK, and there was a heavier reliance on technology. While this presented a learning curve, it also offered growth opportunities. I was in a dynamic environment where innovation was at the forefront of healthcare. This transition, while challenging, felt like a step toward the global vision I had always imagined for myself.

Setting New Goals and Aspiration

Once I had settled in the U.S., my immediate goal was to bring my wife and daughter over as soon as possible. Everything about America was different from what I had experienced in the UK. The capitalist society I found myself in was fast-paced, driven by business and competition, especially in the healthcare industry.

Even the language, though familiar, had its differences; terms like "trousers" became "pants," and "Waterloo" turned into "bathroom." It felt like I had moved from a small island to an enormous continent, and Michigan, where I was based, was unlike any state I had heard of back in London. Everyone seemed to know about California, New York, or Florida, but Michigan was a mystery to most of my friends.

One of the first things I realized was that in Michigan, owning a car was not a luxury but a necessity. Unlike London, which had an extensive public transportation system with the British rail, underground tubes, and buses, Michigan's public transport was severely lacking. This new reality forced me to adjust my lifestyle quickly. Without a car, getting around was impossible, and so owning a vehicle became one of my top priorities.

As I began settling into the U.S., my goals shifted. I was not just here to work but to build something lasting. I aspired to further my education, to climb the ranks of my profession, and to eventually start my own business. I knew the U.S. offered opportunities I had not had in Nigeria or the UK, and I was determined to make the most of it. First, though, I needed to prepare for my U.S. board certification in physiotherapy. I had been hired on a temporary license, but there was a time limit, and passing the board exam was essential for securing my long-term professional future.

In the meantime, I focused on being a good father and husband despite the physical distance between myself and my family. My ambition was to succeed in America and build a future for my family to thrive. The American Dream was within my grasp, and I was ready to work hard to achieve it. The road ahead was challenging, but after all I had been through, from the difficulties in London to this new chapter in the U.S., I knew resilience, faith, and hard work would guide me.

Lessons For Success

Growing Through the Ranks

My ascension through the ranks in my career required me to embrace a significant level of humility. Although my prior education and training in Lagos were comprehensive, I needed to adapt quickly to the sophisticated equipment and different modalities used in the U.S. healthcare system. I was required to sit for board examinations to prove my competencies, ensuring that my qualifications matched U.S. standards. This required persistence, but I viewed each step as a new learning opportunity.

I consistently relied on the wisdom of my colleagues, particularly the physical therapy assistants, who were instrumental in helping me master the advanced equipment and insurance billing practices crucial to my role. I rose through the ranks by focusing on continual growth, learning the technical aspects, and building solid relationships that supported my professional success.

Overcoming Workplace Trials

Adapting to my new environment came with various challenges, especially in communication and cultural integration. My Nigerian accent often made me feel out of place, and there were occasions when patients mistook me for an aide or janitorial staff. Despite these assumptions, I maintained professionalism and focused on the task at hand, using every challenge as a chance to prove my skills and competence.

Another significant hurdle was understanding the U.S. insurance system, which differed significantly from what I was used to in Nigeria and the UK. Learning these systems required patience, but overcoming these trials gave me a deeper understanding of the healthcare system in America and helped me refine my communication and management skills, which are essential for building a successful career.

Cultural Enrichment and Integration

Moving from Nigeria to the UK and then to the U.S. broadened my perspective on cultural diversity. I saw firsthand how my Nigerian heritage could integrate with American customs in America. The cultural differences were vast, but I could draw from both worlds.

In social settings, I embraced my heritage, celebrating Nigerian traditions while participating in American holidays and customs. We found comfort and solidarity within the Nigerian community, creating networks that helped us navigate life in a new country.

Professionally, I discovered that my cultural background and advanced skills allowed me to bridge cultures, provide care, and build relationships with people from diverse backgrounds.

Strengthening Family Bonds

My family remained my most incredible support system through all the professional and personal transitions. Although we may have been scattered across different countries at various times, we always stayed close, whether through regular calls or trips to visit one another. My wife and children were essential in maintaining balance in my life.

As the saying goes, there is nowhere on the planet you would not find a Nigerian community. It did not take long for me to connect with other Nigerians through social interactions, such as parties or invitations from friends. We are all cordial to each other in a foreign land, regardless of our local origins in Nigeria. My wife and daughter joined me in Michigan, USA, two months after our daughter was born.

Global Leadership Insights

Adaptability is Key to Growth

Every professional or personal transition requires flexibility. Embracing new cultures, learning different systems, and adjusting to unexpected challenges are essential for effective global leadership. Success comes from expertise and one's ability to adapt to ever-changing environments.

Humility Leads to Mastery

Climbing through the ranks in a new country demands the humility to learn from those around you, even when you are highly qualified. Seeking advice, asking for help, and learning from assistants or peers can open doors to new knowledge and opportunities. Authentic leadership is grounded in the willingness to be a lifelong learner.

Perseverance Through Trials Builds Resilience

Workplace trials such as cultural differences, bias, or even systems that challenge your professional competency can be daunting. Yet, overcoming these obstacles fosters resilience and strengthens one's ability to thrive. The strength gained from perseverance is a hallmark of global leadership.

Cultural Integration Enhances Leadership

Leaders who integrate their heritage's richness with their new environment's customs stand out. Navigating between cultures allows for greater empathy, understanding, and connection with diverse people. Leaders must honor their roots while embracing the global community they are part of.

Family Support Strengthens Leadership Foundations

Family bonds are a crucial source of strength and balance. As leaders, maintaining close relationships with loved ones helps navigate personal and professional challenges. A strong family foundation can serve as an emotional anchor, allowing leaders to focus on their goals with confidence and stability.

Conclusion

As we conclude "Part 2: Europe – Crossing Borders and Breaking Barriers," it becomes clear that each experience, from navigating the complexities of migration to adapting to a foreign professional landscape, has served as a vital steppingstone. The challenges of adjusting to new cultures, the drive to climb through professional ranks, and the strength to maintain family ties amid transitions have all laid the groundwork for broader horizons. These foundations are more than personal victories. They prepare for stepping into a larger arena.

VENTURE INTO A GLOBAL ENTITY

As we enter "Part 3: USA – Expanding to Global Horizons," the lessons learned in London and the bridges built across Europe will fuel a more ambitious journey. This next stage will realize personal goals and reveal how leadership takes on a global dimension, where influence, vision, and action stretch beyond borders. The opportunities in the United States will catalyze transformation, paving the way for even more remarkable achievements that will focus on leaving a lasting impact on a global scale.

DR. OLAJIDE OKUNROUNMU

PART 3

USA: EXPANDING TO GLOBAL HORIZONS

DR. OLAJIDE OKUNROUNMU

CHAPTER 5

THE BIG MOVE

THE BIG MOVE OFTEN marks a significant turning point in life. More than just a physical relocation, it signifies a fresh chapter filled with possibilities and challenges. Whether it is moving to a new city or country or even embarking on a new career path, such a move demands adaptability, courage, and a willingness to step outside of one's comfort zone.

It is a time for reflection, as familiar surroundings and routines give way to new environments and experiences. While daunting, this transition opens doors to personal growth, new relationships, and opportunities that can reshape one's future and broaden one's horizons. Embracing the big move is a leap toward a renewed sense of purpose and a redefined vision of what lies ahead.

Starting Anew in Michigan

Starting anew is both daunting and exciting. It represents the moment we turn the page and begin a fresh phase in our lives, leaving behind the past and embracing new opportunities. Whether prompted by necessity or choice, starting over requires courage, a willingness to learn, and the resilience to adapt to unfamiliar environments.

It is an opportunity to reassess our goals, refine our values, and carve out a new path that aligns with our evolving vision. Although the future may be uncertain, starting anew offers the chance for reinvention and growth, allowing us to shape our lives with renewed energy and purpose. Each new beginning brings the promise of discovery, transformation, and the potential to achieve something even greater than before.

Arriving in the USA

I arrived in the United States on August 10th, 1990, the same day that Iraq invaded Kuwait. The significance of this event was not lost on me as I stepped onto U.S. soil, thinking about the global unrest juxtaposed with my mission of starting anew. While watching one of the most significant geopolitical shifts unfold, I was entering a new chapter of my life, driven by the promise of more excellent opportunities.

Michigan, a state I had barely heard of back in London, was to be my new home. It was not the glamorous image of New York or California that I had grown up hearing about, but it offered a chance for me to build a stable life and career. The weight of this transition was immense. Everything felt uncertain yet full of possibility.

Initial Adjustments and Copes

Life in Michigan presented its own set of challenges. Coming from my structured life in London, I was quickly introduced to the fast-paced American lifestyle. In my first two months, my hosts and new colleagues ensured I experienced everything American, from dining out regularly to attending movies and engaging in typical social outings. This lifestyle, though exciting, was very different from what I was used to.

In Nigeria and London, meals were often eaten at home, and dining out was rare. I quickly learned that dining out every night could severely strain my finances. Despite earning a good income for a beginner, America's credit-based society was an entirely new system to which I had to adapt. The financial discipline I had developed in Nigeria was being tested, as I lived paycheck to paycheck with no savings to fall back on.

Setting up a new life in the U.S. meant making several down payments on furniture, a car, and even basic living expenses. Given my lack of credit history, the American banking system did not initially extend credit to me. Without a financial safety net, I had to manage every penny carefully.

My wife, who joined me with an H-4 visa, was not allowed to work, which added to the pressure. Adjusting to these new circumstances required careful planning as I juggled the demands of setting up a household, paying off debts, and navigating the American financial system.

Studying The American Health Care System

The American healthcare system was a new world for me, especially compared to the UK and Nigeria. The system's complexity, combined with government-sponsored programs like Medicare and Medicaid alongside various private insurance options, was initially overwhelming. I had to learn quickly how insurance worked in the U.S., as it was an integral part of my professional responsibilities as a physiotherapist. Unlike the National Health Service (NHS) in the UK, where healthcare was universally accessible, the U.S. system was fragmented and required a lot of paperwork and insurance approvals for treatments.

Luckily, I had a lot of support at work. The in-service training provided by my employer was invaluable in helping me navigate this labyrinth. Understanding how insurance companies reimbursed for services was critical to ensuring patients received the care they needed without incurring excessive out-of-pocket costs.

I learned to balance patient care with the administrative side of the profession, ensuring that treatments were effective and financially viable. This was a crucial skill in a country where healthcare was as much about business as it was about care.

Securing Employment and Skilling Up

Six months after arriving in the U.S., I sat for my board examination and passed, officially opening the door for me to integrate fully into the American healthcare system. Passing this exam was a significant milestone, allowing me to practice independently without supervision. My employer was eager to retain my services, especially given the nationwide acute shortage of physical therapists. Their investment in bringing me over from the UK was beginning to pay off, and I could negotiate a raise based on my qualifications and performance.

In addition to securing full-time employment, I began picking up part-time jobs to supplement my income. This allowed me to alleviate some of the financial pressure we were experiencing and expand my skills in different settings. Working in various clinics and hospitals across Michigan exposed me to many patient cases and medical conditions. The diversity of experience I gained in these roles was invaluable in building my expertise and confidence as a healthcare professional.

Family Adjustments

Settling Into a New Environment

When I reflect on the early days in the U.S., settling into a new environment was more than just finding a place to live. It was about building a life from the ground up. Buying our first home in such a short time indicated how deeply ingrained the values of perseverance and hard work were in my wife and me. We had arrived with limited financial resources, and with my wife still unable to work due to her visa status, we relied solely on my income. Yet, despite the constraints, we were determined not to rent forever.

Every dollar had to be stretched. From cutting down on dining out, which seemed so familiar here, to repurposing old furniture from our early days in London, we found ways to make it work. One of the greatest lessons I learned during this time was the importance of financial discipline. America operates on credit, and securing loans or credit cards was challenging without a strong credit history. Yet, we pushed through and managed to save enough for a down payment. The joy of walking into our home was a feeling I will never forget. It was not just a house but a symbol of our resilience and shared dreams.

Welcoming More Children

Our growing family meant new blessings but also new challenges. When our second daughter was born in 1994, followed by our son just 15 months later, it was a period of both joy and fatigue. The dynamic at home shifted significantly suddenly; we had three young children, and every day was a balancing act between work, childcare, and personal time.

My wife, who had recently passed her nursing board exam, started working night shifts to help ease our financial burden. This allowed us to save money on daycare but also meant that we often operated on opposite schedules. I would be finishing my long hours, and she would be heading off to work, and in between, we found pockets of time to spend together as a family.

Looking back, I realize how vital those sacrifices were. The jobs were challenging, the hours were long, and the pay was enough to get by, but it was all for our children's future. Eventually, with our growing needs, we upgraded to a larger five-bedroom house. This home felt like a significant leap forward regarding space and what we could provide for our children. It was not just about having more rooms. It was about providing stability, a nurturing environment, and the sense of accomplishment that comes with hard-earned success.

Parenting and Education

One of the most important legacies I could pass on to my children was the value of a good education. Just as my parents had emphasized the importance of discipline and structure, I wanted my children to have the best foundation possible. This is why we chose to enroll them in private Catholic schools. The controlled environment mirrored what I had experienced growing up in an education that focused on academics and instilled values of respect, integrity, and resilience.

There were times when the financial strain of private schooling felt overwhelming, especially considering the costs of managing a growing family. But my wife and I both agreed that this was non-negotiable. We wanted our children to learn in an environment that fostered discipline and challenged them to excel academically. Watching them embrace their studies with the same dedication I had when I was younger was heartwarming. I often reflected on how education had opened doors for me, and I was committed to ensuring it would do the same for them.

Integration into American Society

Adapting to life in America was gradual, but my children seemed to take to it much more naturally. While my wife and I retained many Nigerian customs, such as speaking our native language at home, cooking traditional meals, and staying involved in the local Nigerian community, our children quickly absorbed American culture.

They effortlessly blended into their school environments, adopting American customs, slang, and interests. I found it fascinating to watch them navigate these two worlds, balancing their Nigerian heritage with the American culture they grew up in.

Integration was more conscious for my wife and me. We had to learn how to balance our values with our new surroundings. The faster pace of life in the U.S., compared to the bustling streets of London or Lagos, took some getting used to.

We were also more mindful of maintaining our cultural identity, ensuring our children understood their origins. We participated in cultural events, maintained ties with other Nigerian families, and celebrated traditional holidays. At the same time, we embraced many aspects of American life, appreciating the diversity, the opportunities, and the freedoms that living in this country offered.

Break New Ground and Overcome Limitations

Literal and figurative Boarders

In our home, boundaries were essential to maintaining order, discipline, and a sense of belonging. We created an environment where each family member understood the importance of structured routines, from daily prayers to shared mealtimes.

These rituals reinforced our family bond and kept us grounded in our values. Our home needed to remain a sanctuary where work stress did not infiltrate our relationships or diminish the quality of our time together.

Weekends became sacred for rest, reinforcing the familial and social connections that shaped our lives. Hosting friends and family members, engaging in cultural and religious activities, and participating in social gatherings kept our ties strong, both with our Nigerian roots and our new American community.

While these symbolic boundaries helped maintain family unity, there were also literal boundaries that we had to navigate. As immigrants, we quickly learned that the boundaries between work and home, American culture and Nigerian traditions, were fluid, and managing them required conscious effort. Adapting to these new environments pushed us to redefine what it meant to belong to two worlds while maintaining our core identity.

The Impact of Immigration

Moving to the U.S. opened opportunities that transformed our standard of living in ways that would have been unimaginable back home in Nigeria. With better employment options came better wages, and this uplift in our financial situation allowed us to afford a lifestyle that elevated our social standing among our friends and family. It was not just about material wealth; immigration provided us with a new outlook on life, where the idea of upward mobility was not a distant dream but a tangible reality for which we could strive.

At the same time, the transition was not always easy. As immigrants, we often work harder and longer hours than ever. The expectations were high, and so were the costs of living. However, what made the difference was the belief that hard work would eventually pay off in America. Unlike in Nigeria, the social systems and opportunities here seemed more accessible.

While challenges persisted, our resilience grew, and the rewards, both personal and financial, were more attainable than they ever had been. Immigration had allowed us to redefine what success looked like, and in doing so, we could carve out a new, more prosperous life for our family.

Cultural Exchange and Integration

One of the most rewarding aspects of our immigration journey was blending the richness of Nigerian culture with the new experiences we encountered in America. We became cultural ambassadors in many ways, sharing our food, traditions, and values with those around us.

Whether it was through community events, church, or the workplace, we often found ourselves in the position of teaching others about our Nigerian heritage. But the learning was not one-sided. The American culture we were now part of taught us much about the power of individualism, freedom of expression, and the importance of community in a different light.

Integrating into American society did not mean abandoning our Nigerian identity but expanding it. We took pride in who we were and where we came from, and it was encouraging to see how many people in our community were eager to learn about our culture.

At the same time, we adopted many American practices, from holiday celebrations to professional work ethics, and blended them with our own. This exchange enriched our lives and allowed us to create a new, hybrid cultural identity that reflected the best of both worlds.

Recognizing and Valuing Opportunities

Upon moving to the U.S., one of the most significant revelations was how opportunities seemed to abound for those willing to seize them.

Unlike in Nigeria, where access to opportunities was often dictated by who you knew or where you came from, America felt like a place where hard work, creativity, and ambition could genuinely pay off. Here, meritocracy ruled that you could succeed if you had the skills and drive. I found this empowering.

In America, I learned to value opportunities differently. Promotions were given based on merit, not nepotism. Doors opened because of hard work, not because of family connections. This shift in mindset changed how I approached my career and my life. I understood that the rewards of this system went beyond just financial stability. They provided a sense of fulfillment and accomplishment.

I also began to recognize opportunities in areas I had never considered before. The possibilities were endless, Whether through investments, further education, or community involvement. The key was to stay focused, work hard, and never lose sight of the goals we had set for ourselves as a family.

Pursuing The American Dream

The American Dream is about living life to the fullest, hoping to achieve your dreams and visions in a nation that offers equal justice, opportunity, and freedom of speech for all. It is a place where democracy operates at its best. America is the land of liberty, where success and achievements are determined by an individual's efforts, not by socioeconomic status or connections.

It is a country where dreams come true for those willing to work hard. The essence of the American Dream lies in the belief that even a poor immigrant like me, with no family support here, can become wealthy and successful through determination, hard work, and personal talents.

Economic Prosperity and Social Mobility

One of the most significant benefits I experienced upon moving to the United States was the economic prosperity that came with my profession. Unlike many of my peers who had migrated earlier and found themselves relying on odd jobs or menial labor to survive, my background in physiotherapy placed me in a much more favorable position.

The field was unknown then, but this was a tremendous advantage. As the demand for skilled physical therapists grew, I found myself in the upper-income bracket, which allowed me to support my family and provided me with social mobility that others in my generation often struggled to achieve.

This newfound financial stability helped me integrate vertically and horizontally into American society, allowing me to associate with professionals in higher social strata. I found myself standing alongside doctors, lawyers, and engineers, people I had once admired from afar.

This rise in status was more than about income; it gave me the confidence to continue growing, to invest in myself, and to pursue the American Dream with full force. What was even more rewarding was knowing that I could offer my children opportunities that I had not had, providing them with a secure foundation for their future.

Hard work and Perseverance

Hard work and perseverance have always been at the core of my upbringing. My parents instilled in me the belief that no matter where I found myself, I had to make the best of the situation. Growing up in a polygamous household taught me resilience. It was not always easy, and I often had to find ways to navigate complex family dynamics. But through it all, I learned that giving up was never an option. This mindset became my guiding principle throughout my journey, especially after moving to America.

Starting fresh in a new country was daunting but not impossible. I kept reminding myself of the values my parents had imparted, such as hard work, integrity, and perseverance. No matter how difficult things became, I always looked for the positive side of life.

I knew that if I kept pushing forward, there would be light at the end of the tunnel. This mentality was critical as I navigated the complexities of my professional and personal life in America. My relentless pursuit of success allowed me to break through barriers and secure a place in the upper echelons of society.

Personal Freedom and Independence

One of the most liberating aspects of coming to America was the sense of personal freedom and independence I gained. For the first time, I was fully responsible for my decisions related to career choices, family finances, and everyday problem-solving. This autonomy allowed me to take control of my life in a way I had never been able to before. I no longer had to rely on extended family or seek approval for my actions. In a sense, I was able to rewrite my narrative.

While I have always valued family, I knew that to succeed, I had to stand on my own two feet. This independence became a defining feature of my time in America. I took the more complex paths, making difficult decisions to ensure the best outcomes for my family.

Whether navigating the complexities of the healthcare industry or managing my household, I took pride in being the one responsible for my success. America allowed me to dream bigger and execute those dreams on my terms.

Education and Self-Improvement

Education has always been a cornerstone of my journey. Still, it was not until a critical moment with one of my daughters that I realized the importance of continuing my personal development. During a heated argument, she blurted out, "Dad, you know nothing." Her words stung, not because they were meant to hurt, but because they exposed a truth I had ignored. I had been so focused on ensuring that my children received the best education possible that I neglected my need for growth.

That moment was a wake-up call. I realized I needed to pursue further education to continue being a robust role model for my children and build a positive foundation for the future.

Rather than simply investing in my children's academic journeys, I had to invest in my own. I began seeking postgraduate opportunities to further my knowledge and expand my horizons. Education was not just about gaining qualifications. It was about improving myself as a father, a professional, and a leader.

Global Leadership Highlights

Resilience in the Face of Change

True leaders can adapt to new environments and thrive, even when faced with significant personal and professional challenges. Relocating to a new country and starting from scratch requires strength and resilience. Leaders must be able to navigate the unknown, staying grounded in their values while remaining open to new opportunities.

Hard Work as a Pathway to Prosperity

Hard work is a crucial ingredient in achieving success. In any environment, especially in a country like the U.S., where opportunities abound for those who seek them, hard work becomes a foundation upon which dreams are built. Leaders should embrace the reality that personal effort, determination, and perseverance can break down barriers and create pathways to more significant achievements.

Leveraging Education for Growth

Formal and informal education are vital tools for personal and professional growth. Leaders recognize the value of continuous learning for themselves and those around them. Investing in education ensures leaders remain relevant, adaptable, and prepared to face future challenges.

Cultural Adaptation and Integration

Influential leaders can harmonize different cultural perspectives, blending their heritage with the norms of their new environments. This ability to integrate culturally while maintaining one's identity is critical to global leadership. By embracing diversity and learning from new cultures, leaders can expand their influence and foster meaningful connections across borders.

The Power of Independence and Self-Reliance

Personal freedom and independence are key elements in leadership. The ability to take control of one's own life and make decisions that shape the future demonstrates leadership at its core. Leaders thrive when they take ownership of their paths, relying on their abilities to solve problems and create opportunities without overly depending on external support.

Pursuing the Dream with Integrity

The American Dream teaches that anyone can succeed with hard work, perseverance, and integrity. Regardless of circumstances, leaders who uphold these values inspire others to believe in their potential. By staying focused on their goals, maintaining integrity, and embracing the opportunities available, leaders can carve out their success and inspire others to do the same.

Conclusion

As the challenges of starting anew began to shape my perspective, it became clear that this move was not just a transition but the beginning of something far greater. Striding into unfamiliar territory, personally and professionally, opened doors to possibilities I had not envisioned before.

This relocation symbolized more than just a change of address; it laid the groundwork for expanding my ambitions beyond local boundaries. The experiences gathered from these early days would later fuel the vision of growing from a local presence to a global entity and how local roots can transform into a global influence, driving growth and making a lasting impact.

CHAPTER 6

FROM A LOCAL TO GLOBAL ENTITY

Entrepreneurial Ventures

Founding Care Plus Physical Therapy

I did not set out to create Care Plus Physical Therapy from scratch. Instead, I partnered with Mr. Moe, the original owner who purchased the business, while I brought the professional expertise needed to elevate the practice. This partnership was a significant turning point in my career. It introduced me to a different realm of healthcare practice, specifically Outpatient clinical care with a focus on orthopedic conditions.

What made this venture unique was the patient population we served and the professionals I had to collaborate with daily. Given the types of patients, we often treated, those dealing with workplace injuries or car accidents, I interacted with numerous attorneys, adding a layer of complexity to the practice. I had to quickly adapt to managing the medical and legal aspects of patient care, which helped me develop new skills and grow professionally in ways I had not anticipated.

Services and Specializations

At Care Plus, we specialize in various services, focusing on orthopedic rehabilitation. Our patients primarily come to us with musculoskeletal issues, whether post-surgery recovery, chronic conditions, or acute injuries. This allows us to serve a broad patient base, ranging from athletes and manual laborers to accident survivors.

As the outpatient therapist in charge, I quickly realized the importance of staying ahead in my field. To be effective, I needed to keep abreast of new developments within my scope of practice, ensuring that I could anticipate and accurately predict the conditions and symptoms my patients presented. Practicing in such a specialized environment meant no room for error; you must be fully prepared to handle various complex cases.

My post-graduate degree became a crucial asset, allowing me to embrace Evidence-Based Practice fully. This approach enabled me to incorporate the latest research and clinical advancements into my treatments, ensuring every patient received care rooted in the most up-to-date medical knowledge. Evidence-based practice was not just a concept;

it became the foundation of our services at Care Plus. Using this method, I could offer personalized care plans that prioritized immediate recovery and long-term wellness for my patients.

Patient-Centered Approach

At the core of Care Plus Physical Therapy was a patient-centered approach that guided everything we did. Communication with patients had to be a top priority to provide the best care. Over time, I developed strategies to improve how we communicated with patients, promote our practice, and retain our patient base, ensuring we did not lose them to competitors. In the competitive field of physical therapy, patient retention was crucial, and this meant going beyond just clinical care—patients needed to feel valued and supported throughout their recovery journey.

Part of our approach involved navigating the often-complex relationships with various insurance companies. Ensuring proper reimbursement for our services was an ongoing challenge. We often faced declined billings, but I took it upon myself to advocate for our clinic. On numerous occasions, I worked directly with our attorneys to defend our claims in court, ensuring that we received the reimbursements that our patients and our practice deserved.

In these moments, I took on multiple roles within the clinic. From clinical decisions to legal advocacy, I had to become the Alpha and Omega of the practice, responsible for every facet of its operation. This holistic approach ensured that our patients received the best care and solidified Care Plus as a trusted name in the community.

Community Impact

Beyond providing clinical care, Care Plus Physical Therapy became deeply rooted in the community we served. The clinic was situated in a Muslim-dominated community, with many of our patients coming from countries like Iraq, Iran, Saudi Arabia, and Kuwait. Understanding and respecting our patients' cultural and religious practices was crucial to our success. I took it upon myself to learn about the community's faiths, morals, and ideals. This knowledge allowed me to create a more welcoming and culturally sensitive environment for our patients.

One significant adjustment was establishing a separate room within the clinic where patients could have private prayer sessions. Many of our patients prayed five times daily, and providing them with a space to practice their faith ensured they felt comfortable and respected while receiving care. We were also mindful of scheduling, avoiding appointments on Fridays or key religious days, and respecting fasting periods that could last for weeks.

In addition, we recognized the language barriers some patients faced, particularly those with limited English comprehension. To bridge this gap, we employed clinical practice language interpreters, ensuring that all patients, regardless of their language skills, could fully understand their treatment plans and engage in their recovery process. This cultural sensitivity and patient support helped us build strong, trusting relationships within the community, further solidifying Care Plus as a trusted and inclusive healthcare provider.

Overcoming Obstacles

Challenges and Achievements

Running an outpatient clinic like Care Plus Physical Therapy faced its fair share of challenges. On any given day, I had to navigate the complexities of managing a diverse patient base with various personalities, cultural backgrounds, and expectations. Conflicts would arise between patients or staff members, and as the leader, it fell to me to maintain an atmosphere of professionalism and care.

In healthcare, emotions often run high, especially when patients are dealing with pain, frustration, or slow recovery. Ensuring our clinic provided a space where patients felt understood, respected, and valued was critical. That required a delicate balance; on the one hand, we needed to maintain boundaries, but on the other, empathy was just as important.

Managing staff was not just another task but an integral part of our patient care strategy. It was another essential component of running the practice. Many of our junior staff members were new to healthcare. While they were enthusiastic, they often lacked the experience needed to handle the daily pressures of a busy clinic. To address this, we implemented regular staff training sessions focusing on technical skills and healthcare's softer, interpersonal aspects.

These sessions emphasized the importance of creating boundaries between professionalism and socialization. We worked on punctuality, communication, and stress management to avoid the burnout many young healthcare workers face in high-stress environments. This ongoing professional development was crucial to ensuring the clinic operated smoothly while supporting the personal growth of our employees.

Through these challenges, we achieved many milestones. Our retention rates improved because of the quality of care we provided, our relationships with our patients, and the trust we fostered within the community.

Over time, Care Plus became a trusted name in the region, one of the most outstanding achievements, knowing that our practice had a meaningful impact on the lives of those we served.

Navigating Professional Hurdles

Staying ahead of professional hurdles and committing to excellence was essential in a rapidly evolving healthcare landscape. Like many healthcare fields, the physical therapy industry constantly advances with new research, technologies, and treatment methodologies. For a clinic to remain competitive and relevant, we must stay at the cutting edge of these developments and set the pace for others to follow.

I took it upon myself to consistently stay abreast of clinical updates through self-study or attending industry conferences. These gatherings provided invaluable insights into the latest trends in patient care and allowed me to network with other professionals facing similar challenges. I focused on advancements in evidence-based practices that could enhance patient outcomes and improve our clinic's reputation as a forward-thinking provider.

However, clinical expertise was only part of the equation. A significant hurdle was mastering the intricacies of the insurance billing system. The U.S. healthcare industry operates on a complex web of insurance plans, each with its rules, coverage guidelines, and reimbursement processes. One of our biggest frustrations as a practice was dealing with denied claims. These denials affected the clinic's financial health and delayed critical care for our patients.

To mitigate these issues, I dedicated significant time to studying the insurance landscape, learning the ins and outs of various billing methods, and optimizing our processes to ensure smoother transactions. I also frequently worked alongside attorneys, advocating for our patients' right to coverage, particularly in cases where claims were wrongfully denied. This added a legal dimension to my role that, while challenging, became an asset in keeping the clinic financially sound.

Professional Achievements

Amidst these challenges, I achieved several key professional milestones that further solidified my expertise and the clinic's success. One of the most significant was completing my postgraduate studies. Returning to school while managing a full-time clinic and continuing home care visits was no easy task, but it was a necessary step to expand my knowledge and credentials. My advanced education allowed me to offer more specialized services at Care Plus and gave me the confidence to implement new treatment protocols and management strategies.

Beyond my academic accomplishments, my professional achievements were reflected in the clinic's growth. We began offering a more comprehensive range of services, reaching a broader demographic, and making strides in outpatient care that set us apart from our competitors.

The successful application of my post-graduate learning into our clinical setting enabled us to handle more complex cases, and we saw a steady increase in patient referrals, particularly for orthopedic conditions that required specialized rehabilitation. Over time, Care Plus became known for its patient-centered approach and ability to handle challenging medical cases with precision and care.

Personal Fulfillment

On the personal front, the years between 2009 and 2017 were a period of profound transformation and introspection. The 2008 financial crisis hit us hard, and the fallout reverberated throughout our family. We faced the heartbreaking reality of nearly losing our home, and I was forced to give up Okuns Plaza, the commercial building where I had invested my savings.

The building was in a high-crime area of Detroit, which exposed us to constant burglaries, making it impossible to maintain the business. The mounting costs, taxes, and economic downturn led to the foreclosure of the building—a devastating financial and emotional blow.

The sudden shift in our financial situation significantly impacted our family dynamic. My children, used to a certain level of comfort, began to question whether we were "broke." It was a difficult time, and my wife and children even considered selling our home in Wayne, thinking it was beneath our social status.

But instead of succumbing to despair, I chose to focus on reinvention. We sold our Southfield house with its high mortgage and downsized to our home in Wayne, which we could purchase outright. While it felt like a step back then, it was a crucial move toward financial stability and personal autonomy.

During these years, I completed my postgraduate education, found a renewed sense of purpose, and laid the groundwork for future growth. Despite the external challenges, my children thrived in their new schools, securing scholarships for college and reaffirming our choices.

I also deepened my involvement with Prime Investment, an investment club where I served as the investment manager. Through intelligent investing and careful management, I leveraged my gains to purchase a vacation home in Georgia, a testament to resilience and long-term planning.

In retrospect, the hardships we endured were a turning point. They forced me to realign my goals and focus on the authenticity and purpose that had always driven me. The economic setback was not just a period of loss—it was an opportunity for growth and became the foundation for a more secure and fulfilled future.

Business Growth

Taking Stock of Key Milestones and Triumphs

Looking back at my milestones and triumphs, I often reflect on my mantra: "Any situation does not move me because they are subject to change." No matter the challenges or obstacles I have faced, I have always kept my faith, trusting that God controls my destiny, as the book of Psalm 46:1 reminds me. I have never let circumstances dictate my direction, choosing instead to walk by faith and not by sight. This mindset has been vital to navigating personal and professional trials, allowing me to turn setbacks into steppingstones.

One of the most significant milestones in my journey was establishing and growing Care Plus Physical Therapy. Partnering with Mr. Moe to bring my professional expertise to the clinic was a considerable achievement. Through hard work and innovation, I played a crucial role in shaping the clinic into a reputable healthcare provider. It was not just a place for physical therapy—it was a beacon of personalized care and community engagement. As we expanded our services and built a patient base, the clinic became a model for how dedication and vision could create something impactful.

Beyond healthcare, my ventures into real estate and investments were also pivotal. I still remember my father's lessons about delaying gratification and saving for the future. Although we rented houses in Lagos growing up, my father was among the first in our community to build properties in Oshodi and Maza-Maza. I often wondered why we did not move into one of his houses, but in time, I realized that he was instilling in me the value of delayed rewards. Today, one of his houses still provides for my family, a testament to his foresight and wisdom.

His foundations enabled me to explore financial opportunities, and my time with the Prime Investment Club of Michigan was instrumental in developing my financial intelligence. I learned to evaluate stocks and global markets, investing heavily in the American stock market, Nigeria, and Ghana. These experiences bolstered my financial position and allowed me to diversify my investments, creating multiple income streams.

Understanding the Market

My father's lessons on delaying gratification profoundly impacted how I approached my financial decisions. He never spoiled me with money but gave me something more valuable: financial wisdom. He showed me the importance of not spending today what I would need for tomorrow. Growing up, I watched as he built rental properties while we continued to rent, and only later did I understand the strategy behind his decisions. He was creating wealth for the future, not just for himself but for future generations.

This early exposure to real estate investment became one of the first pillars of my financial education. My father's approach to building and managing properties left a lasting impression, and I continued by investing in real estate myself. Later, joining the Prime Investment Club of Michigan allowed me to expand my financial knowledge further, particularly in stock market investments.

Working with like-minded individuals, I learned to evaluate companies, track market trends, and make informed decisions. This practical exposure to financial intelligence gave me the confidence to take calculated risks, including investing in the Ghana Stock Exchange, which a close friend, Sam Gbadamosi, introduced me to.

Over time, I expanded my ventures beyond real estate and stocks, exploring retail businesses such as hall rentals, equipment rentals, and even medical equipment sales. This diversification has been critical in weathering financial downturns and ensuring long-term sustainability across all my business ventures.

Legal and Regulatory Compliance

I have always understood the importance of legal and regulatory compliance in every business I have been involved in. One of my early lessons was that having a great idea or a profitable venture is not enough. You need to ensure that you are operating within the boundaries of the law.

To this end, I have always relied on the expertise of accountants and lawyers to help guide my business decisions. Whether it was ensuring compliance with city, state, or national regulations, these professionals have been invaluable in helping me establish solid foundations for my ventures.

From zoning laws in real estate to healthcare compliance in the physical therapy clinic, I took every step to protect my businesses from unnecessary legal issues. Staying compliant has allowed me to focus on growth, knowing that the operational aspects of my companies are secure and well-managed.

The Creation of OKUNSGLOBAL

The creation of OKUNSGLOBAL was a natural evolution of the business ventures I had been involved in over the years. It began as Okuns Ventures, Inc. in Michigan in 2003. Over time, it grew into a more diversified entity with other business interests, such as Care Plus Physical Therapy and Okuns Investment, Nigeria Ltd.

With our eventual relocation from Michigan to Georgia in 2017 and the further expansion of our ventures in Nigeria, the business transformed into OKUNS GLOBAL, Inc. This new entity represented not just the growth of my business but a consolidation of everything I had worked for over the years.

OKUNS GLOBAL now operates as an international business, with interests spanning multiple industries and countries. Our vision is to continue expanding, leveraging the experiences and lessons learned from years of entrepreneurship to build a global brand that serves communities and contributes to economic growth on an international scale. The journey from local ventures to a global entity has been filled with challenges, but it has also been gratifying, and I look forward to seeing where this next phase takes us.

Blueprint for Global Expansion

Our vision and goal is to establish Okuns as a global brand recognized as a leader in all our ventures, much like Ford, Walmart, and Mercedes in their respective industries.

Cultivate a Global Mindset

A crucial element in building a global business is cultivating a global mindset, thinking beyond borders, and embracing different cultures, ideas, and perspectives. One early example was when an American woman rented a shop from us at our shopping complex in Abeokuta, Ogun State, Nigeria.

Despite never setting foot on Nigerian soil, she established a successful barbering salon and boutique called Yanda's Boutique. Her only prior experience in Africa was attending a coworker's wedding in Sierra Leone, yet this was enough to spark her interest in creating a business in Nigeria. That experience is the handiwork of our global mindset, where we want to connect and interact with people with other cultures and customs.

This experience taught me the value of cultural exchange and how much can be accomplished when you open yourself to the world. In many ways, it reaffirmed my commitment to developing a global mindset in all my ventures. I learned that people from different backgrounds and cultures can collaborate effectively when given the opportunity.

It was not just about conducting business locally, connecting with the global market, and using those connections to grow and learn. The global economy requires companies to be adaptable and culturally aware, and these principles guide my approach to business expansion.

Establish Strategic Partnerships

In today's interconnected world, no business can succeed alone. To truly expand globally, we understood that building strategic partnerships was essential. Our long-term goal has always been to leverage our strengths and resources by collaborating with like-minded businesses and individuals worldwide. These partnerships provide access to new markets and enable us to pool resources, share knowledge, and expand our reach in ways that would be impossible to do alone.

We aim to market our business and brand globally by forming strategic alliances. The key to successful partnerships is ensuring that both parties bring something valuable. Whether expanding into new geographical regions, diversifying product offerings, or integrating new technologies, these partnerships will allow us to scale effectively and sustainably. We focus on building relationships that will stand the test of time, ensuring we remain competitive and forward-thinking in the ever-changing global marketplace.

Build a Personal Brand

Branding is one of the most critical aspects of creating a legacy in business. For us, the journey began in Michigan, where we established Okuns Plaza, an event center located on Dundee Street in Detroit. Initially, it was a small venture, but it grew into a household name known for hosting events and providing top-notch services over time. Our name, "Okuns," was an abbreviation of Okunrounmu, which became the identity that people associated with quality and reliability. Even after relocating to Georgia, the name "Okuns" followed us; to this day, it is what most people call us.

The power of personal branding primarily drove our success. We worked tirelessly to build our reputation through various channels, including radio advertisements and social media. We understand that building a brand is not just about offering a product or service; it is about building trust and creating an emotional connection with your customers.

We cultivated this by delivering exceptional service and maintaining a solid presence in the community, ensuring that our brand was recognizable and respected.

Maintaining this personal brand identity remains at the forefront of our expansion strategy as we grow.

Leverage Technology

As the world continues to shift toward a more digitally connected economy, the role of technology in business expansion cannot be overstated. We recognized early on that leveraging technology would be critical to advancing our brand. With the advent of social media platforms such as Facebook, Google, LinkedIn, and Twitter, we have reached wider audiences and created a more significant impact. These platforms allow us to share our stories, connect with clients, and promote our services across the globe.

As we expand, we plan to explore the potential of digital publishing and other forms of online engagement. Our vision includes sharing our story through books, eBooks, and video content, which would allow us to reach a broader audience and inspire others with our journey.

Furthermore, we are considering using video conferences and webinars to connect with partners and clients globally in real time. By embracing these technologies in the future, we aim to build a more substantial presence in the global market and create new opportunities for growth and collaboration.

Global Leadership Insights

Embrace a Global Mindset

Authentic leadership in a global context requires a mindset that transcends local boundaries. By embracing different cultures, customs, and perspectives, leaders can foster meaningful relationships and open new avenues for business. Global leaders understand that the world is interconnected and actively seek opportunities to learn and grow through these connections.

Build Strategic Partnerships

Leadership is not about going alone. Successful leaders recognize the power of collaboration and are willing to build strategic alliances that complement their strengths. In doing so, they create pathways for growth that extend far beyond their immediate reach. Global expansion relies on these partnerships, allowing businesses to scale efficiently while tapping into new markets.

Develop a Strong Personal Brand

A solid personal brand is essential for any leader aiming to make a lasting impact. It is not just about what you do but how you are perceived by your community, clients, and industry. A recognizable and trusted brand opens doors and builds loyalty, making expanding into new territories and industries easier. Leaders who invest in their brands are better equipped to navigate global business challenges.

Leverage Technology for Growth

In the modern world, technology is a powerful tool for scaling businesses and reaching new audiences. Leaders who effectively leverage technology can connect with clients, partners, and teams worldwide in real-time. By exploring future technological advancements whether through digital content, webinars, or social media leaders can position their businesses for global success.

Adapt to Legal and Regulatory Frameworks

Navigating different countries' legal and regulatory landscapes is crucial for global leadership. Leaders who ensure compliance at every level protect their businesses from risks and build a foundation for sustainable growth. Professionals such as lawyers and accountants can assist leaders in focusing on expansion while knowing that their ventures are legally secure.

Conclusion

Settling into a new life in the United States was far from simple, yet it was a defining period filled with lessons in resilience and adaptability. The early challenges of adjusting to a new culture, navigating the complexities of the American healthcare system, and establishing a financial foundation were not just tests of endurance but growth opportunities. These experiences built a sturdy platform to support future ventures and open doors to personal and professional success.

As we turn the page, we focus on pursuing greater ambitions and entrepreneurial endeavors. What began as a process of adaptation now becomes a journey of expansion and vision, where the lessons of the past drive the pursuit of a broader global impact.

CHAPTER 7

THE IMMIGRANT'S DIARIES

THE EXPERIENCE OF AN immigrant is often one of immense challenge and unparalleled opportunity. It involves leaving behind the familiar for the unknown, navigating new cultural landscapes, and redefining one's sense of identity in a foreign land. Immigrants often find themselves in a delicate balancing act, striving to preserve their roots while adapting to the new realities of their adopted home.

While difficult, this process is also transformative, reshaping personal and professional goals. Through perseverance and resilience, immigrants build new lives that contribute to their success and their new communities' social and economic fabric. These diaries are stories of reinvention, persistence, and the unique perspectives that only the immigrant experience can bring.

The Role of Faith and Personal Values

For immigrants, faith and personal values become essential pillars that provide stability amid the uncertainty of adjusting to new environments. Faith is a source of strength, offering hope and reassurance during adversity or cultural dissonance. It helps individuals maintain a sense of purpose, even when the future feels uncertain. On the other hand, personal values act as a moral compass, guiding decisions and actions in a foreign land where familiar norms may no longer apply.

In traversing the convolutions of immigration, faith and values ensure that individuals remain connected to their roots while adapting to new circumstances. They foster resilience, grounding immigrants in principles that transcend geographic boundaries. Whether overcoming personal challenges or making ethical decisions in professional endeavors, faith and values guide them toward a path of integrity and purpose, shaping their journeys toward success while maintaining a sense of responsibility for themselves and their communities.

The Genesis of Faith

Faith has been the bedrock of everything I do since my earliest years. Raised in a Christian household, I learned faith turns ordinary men into extraordinary achievers. My father's deep commitment to his faith and active church role influenced our family life.

Growing up, I learned early that faith was not merely about attending Sunday service or reciting prayers but about a profound belief in something more significant that guided all aspects of life. The Bible verse, "Faith is the substance of things hoped for, the evidence of things not seen" (Hebrews 11:1), became an anchor for me.

I saw firsthand how my father used faith to shape the way he worked, parented, and led in our community. He instilled in us the belief that faith turns dreams into reality, even when the path ahead is unclear. As the firstborn, I was expected to set an example, and faith was one of the strongest pillars on which I built my life.

My faith made me believe that no obstacle was too significant and no challenge was too impossible. Faith was my anchor whether in school, where I faced academic pressure, or later in life during personal or professional crises. This foundation prepared me for the trials and triumphs that lay ahead.

Faith In Times of Adversity

Faith has been my greatest ally during difficult times. Over the years, I have learned that adversity is inevitable, but how we handle these challenges defines our character.

Through faith, I found strength when faced with disappointments, setbacks, and loss.

From early on, I had to cope with the demands placed on me as the firstborn, which shaped me into a person who would face adversity head-on. It was not always easy, but my faith allowed me to see beyond the hardship, trusting that every challenge had a purpose.

One of the most significant adversities I faced was when I did not meet the score requirement for my first choice of course to study medicine. This setback could have derailed my ambition, but I leaned on my faith to persevere. I chose to press forward, embracing that God had a different plan for me.

That plan unfolded when I later pursued physiotherapy, a decision that led me to a fulfilling career. During other challenging periods, such as financial difficulties or personal losses, I found solace in believing that God was walking with me, guiding my every step. My faith empowered me to continue, even when I did not understand the "why" behind the struggle.

Faith In Decision Making

Faith is instrumental in every decision I make, from career choices to financial investments. Growing up in a household where every major family decision was accompanied by prayer, I learned to seek God's guidance.

This practice of involving faith in decision-making became second nature to me. As the Bible says, "In all your ways, acknowledge Him, and He will direct your paths" (Proverbs 3:6).

Whether I was choosing a career path, deciding where to invest my time and money, or making personal life decisions, I always turned to God first. This approach has given me peace of mind, knowing that my choices are not based solely on my understanding but are guided by a higher power.

One critical example was my decision to pursue physiotherapy after initially wanting to study medicine. While it was not my first choice, I felt a sense of peace after much prayer and reflection. This faith-driven decision opened doors I had not anticipated and led to a rewarding career.

Similarly, I made significant decisions in my personal life, such as purchasing real estate or navigating family challenges based on my faith. Trusting God's plan has allowed me to approach decision-making confidently, even when outcomes are uncertain.

Faith in Action - Investment

As the saying goes, faith without action is dead, and this principle has guided my approach to investment. While I always prioritize faith in my decisions, I learned that it also requires discernment, preparation, and action.

Over the years, I have made various investments in real estate, stocks, and other ventures, some of which succeeded and others that did not go as planned. However, faith taught me that even when things do not turn out as expected, there is always a lesson to be learned.

One such instance was when I purchased the Okuns Plaza in Detroit. My decision was based on an emotional response to being evicted from a banquet hall, and while my faith encouraged me to pursue the investment, I did not do my due diligence.

The building was in a high-crime area, which created numerous challenges. Despite the difficulties, I trusted God would guide me through the process. Although the outcome was not ideal, the experience taught me valuable lessons about faith, emotion, and business decisions.

I also apply faith in my stock trading and other investments. While I strive to make calculated decisions, an element of faith is always involved, especially when entering uncertain markets.

In real estate and business, I have learned to put God first, trusting that He will bless my efforts and help me discern between wise and unwise investments. Faith has given me the strength to take risks and taught me humility when those risks do not yield the expected results.

Importance of Family and Relationships

Family and relationships form the cornerstone of our lives, shaping who we are and influencing the paths we choose. They create a sense of belonging, offering a foundation that keeps us grounded through life's complexities. These connections give us emotional strength and serve as a source of inspiration and wisdom as we pursue our goals. Whether through shared experiences, mutual understanding, or unconditional support, the bonds we forge with those closest to us are integral to our personal and professional growth.

Below, we explore the key benefits that family and relationships bring to our lives:

Emotional Support

Family has always been the bedrock of my emotional support. My nuclear family, wife, and children have consistently given me the strength to face the world. Coming home to a well-cultured, balanced, and supportive family has been a pillar in my life, particularly during trying times.

My wife, Yemisi, is the heart of this structure. Her humility, gentleness, and resilience have been my sanctuary. She has remained steadfast through all the highs and lows of my career, especially when I felt overwhelmed by the expectations set on me. In their way, my children have also contributed to this emotional anchor, providing joy and motivation that kept me pushing forward.

Knowing that your family is there for you unconditionally cannot be overstated. My family has been my emotional compass, whether during the early challenges of adapting to life in a foreign country or the later demands of building and running multiple businesses.

Cultural Preservation and Adaptation

Preserving cultural identity has always been a key value in our family, even as we navigated the complexities of living in the United States. My wife and I initially found embracing certain aspects of American culture challenging. The idea of frequent dining out, going to beaches for vacations, and participating in what seemed like leisurely activities felt foreign.

In contrast, our vacations were typically centered around visiting Nigeria, reconnecting with extended family, and offering gifts, a tradition we valued deeply. However, this often led to more stress than relaxation, leaving us returning to the U.S. more tired than refreshed.

Despite these struggles, we managed to find a balance over time, integrating some aspects of the American lifestyle while still preserving our Nigerian roots. This adaptation allowed us to blend the best of both worlds, creating a cultural synergy that enriched our lives and our children's.

Social Integration

Social integration in the United States posed its challenges. Although I found myself integrating more seamlessly into mainstream American culture, there remained a gap in my ability to embrace African American culture fully. This created a communication gap between myself and some of my African American counterparts.

My upbringing in Nigeria, shaped by its distinct cultural norms, placed me in a unique position when it came to connecting with different racial and ethnic groups in America. While I easily mingled with other immigrant communities, adapting to the local nuances of African American culture required more effort and understanding.

Despite these challenges, I maintained my core values, always striving to bridge gaps wherever I could, understanding that social integration is a continuous process that takes time and patience.

Economic Stability

The lessons from my childhood, particularly the emphasis on living within one's means, have profoundly impacted how I approach economic stability. My parents instilled in me the importance of frugality and careful financial planning, which have stayed with me throughout my life, guiding me through prosperous and challenging financial periods. The ability to adapt during economic downturns, whether due to inflation or low employment periods, has been a crucial part of my success. Early on, I learned to prioritize delayed gratification, saving more, and spending wisely. This discipline laid the foundation for my later achievements in business and investment. These early lessons, rooted in family values, equipped me to navigate the complex financial landscapes of Nigeria and the United States.

Attaining Financial Independence

Understanding the US Financial System

Attaining financial independence begins with a solid understanding of the economic system in which one operates. Upon arriving in the United States, I quickly realized that the American economy, dominated by capitalism, operates on a fundamentally different level than what I had experienced in Nigeria.

In the U.S., the financial system is primarily shaped by supply and demand, with the market determining the value of goods, services, and assets. With its complex web of regulations, taxation, and monetary policies, this free-market enterprise system took some time to comprehend fully.

As I dove deeper into the nuances of this system, it became evident that the U.S. dollar dictated not only the local economy but also significantly influenced global trade. Learning to navigate within a system driven by capitalism meant adopting principles aligned with maximizing opportunities presented by market forces.

This realization was crucial in shaping my financial habits and decisions. Understanding how this system worked allowed me to better prepare for investment opportunities and develop strategies that capitalized on the inherent strengths of a free-market economy. Over time, this knowledge became the foundation for my pursuit of financial independence.

Budgeting and Managing Finances

One of the most pivotal moments in my financial education came when I encountered the intricacies of budgeting and managing my finances in the U.S. Moving to a new country, particularly one with a vastly different economic system, required a steep learning curve. I had always believed I had a good grasp on money management.

Still, owning my first house in Oak Park, Michigan, opened my eyes to the complexities of taxation and financial obligations in the U.S. When I filed my first yearly tax return, I was under the impression that I would receive a tax refund, something I had anticipated eagerly. Instead, I owed money to the government, a revelation that stunned me.

This was my financial awakening in a capitalist society. My accountant explained that my income had surpassed the deductions and depreciation threshold, which meant I was liable for higher taxes. This experience highlighted the importance of fully understanding tax laws and how financial management extends beyond simple saving and spending.

Budgeting became more than just a monthly activity; it became a strategic planning process for long-term financial health, ensuring I accounted for all tax liabilities and financial obligations. The lessons learned from that early experience have continued to shape how I manage my finances today, ensuring that I maintain a balanced approach to spending, saving, and investing.

Saving and Investment

Saving has always been a core part of my financial philosophy, something deeply ingrained in me from my family's teachings. Growing up, I was taught the value of creating wealth for myself and future generations. My paternal grandfather and father instilled in me the principle of giving and building a legacy that outlives you. This is why saving, for me, is not just about accumulating wealth but ensuring that the wealth I generate can serve as a foundation for my children and their children.

Alongside saving, I have always been a calculated risk-taker. Part of financial independence involves venturing into new and emerging markets and being willing to explore the unknown for the possibility of significant returns. In recent years, I have dabbled in speculative investments like cryptocurrency and the burgeoning marijuana industry.

While some of these investments carry considerable risk, they are part of a broader investment strategy to diversify my portfolio. I follow strict investment plans, ensuring that I do not invest impulsively but make informed decisions based on thorough research and market trends. Whether investing in stocks, real estate, or new ventures, my approach is disciplined, always with an eye toward long-term growth and wealth creation.

Accessing Financial Resources

One of the keys to attaining financial independence lies in the ability to access and effectively utilize financial resources. Over the years, I have learned to leverage the income generated from my rental properties to diversify into other financial assets. Retained earnings from my building rentals have been an invaluable resource, enabling me to invest in various avenues such as treasury bills, stocks, and even a personal money-lending business that finances individual and business needs.

Through these retained earnings, I have expanded my financial reach by investing in traditional financial instruments and actively participating in community financing. Lending money to others is not just an act of generating interest income. It is a way of giving back and supporting local entrepreneurs and small business owners who may not have access to traditional forms of credit. In doing so, I have created additional streams of income that contribute to my overall financial independence while fostering relationships within my community.

By accessing and wisely utilizing these financial resources, I have built a stable foundation that allows me to continue growing my wealth while maintaining a solid financial footing, even during uncertain economic times. The ability to reinvest profits and make sound financial decisions has been instrumental in my journey toward financial freedom.

Tips For Aspiring Immigrants

Brace Yourself for The Challenge

Immigrating to a new country, particularly one as vast and diverse as the United States can be an overwhelming experience filled with countless challenges. For many immigrants, finding affordable housing is one of the first hurdles to overcome. Cities like New York, Los Angeles, and Chicago are notorious for high living costs, making it difficult for newcomers to secure a place that fits their budget. Beyond that, communication barriers can be daunting, especially for those not fluent in English. This creates additional difficulties when securing employment, interacting daily, or navigating essential services such as healthcare and transportation.

Transportation, for instance, can be a significant issue for immigrants who relocate to cities with limited public transport infrastructure. The ease of getting around, which many may have taken for granted in their home countries, can become a significant obstacle.

The challenge is magnified for those raising families in a foreign environment where cultural differences, new educational systems, and unfamiliar community dynamics present constant stress. Despite these difficulties, understanding that the process will be challenging is the first step toward preparing mentally and emotionally for the road ahead.

Build a Support Network

It is often said that no one is an island, and this is particularly true for immigrants. Building a solid support network is beneficial and essential for survival and success in a new country. Immigrants should prioritize connecting with family, friends, neighbors, work colleagues, and others who can provide guidance, advice, and companionship. A network's emotional support is invaluable, especially during the early stages of settling in.

Local community associations, churches, and immigrant groups often serve as havens where individuals can find others who understand their struggles. These organizations offer more than just emotional support; they usually provide essential resources like language classes, job placement services, and advice on navigating local systems.

The advent of social media has revolutionized the way immigrants can connect with others. Platforms like Facebook, LinkedIn, and TikTok allow newcomers to join groups focusing on their specific needs, whether finding housing, securing jobs, or simply meeting others in similar circumstances. Online networks can extend support across cities, states, or even countries, creating a lifeline for immigrants who feel isolated or overwhelmed.

Leverage Education and Skills

Education is one of the most excellent tools immigrants can use to integrate into their new environment and improve their chances of success. Many immigrants arrive with valuable skills and qualifications but may need to adapt or enhance those skills to align with the needs of their host country.

Joining student groups, networking with others in the same field, and enrolling in technical courses can significantly ease this transition. By learning together and sharing knowledge, immigrants can quickly bridge gaps in their education or skills, saving time and money.

Investing in education, whether through formal university programs or informal learning, opens doors to better employment opportunities. For many, obtaining certifications or degrees recognized in the U.S. is critical to building a stable, successful life.

Beyond formal education, immigrants should also network with colleagues and friends with technical or industry-specific expertise. The willingness to learn and adapt is vital, as new skills and knowledge can help fast-track career growth and enhance job security.

Pursue Entrepreneurship as an Immigrant

For good reason, the entrepreneurial spirit is alive and well among immigrants. Immigrants built the United States, and many of its most successful businesses were started by people who came from abroad with little more than an idea and a willingness to work hard. Pursuing entrepreneurship is not only a way to achieve financial independence but also a method for contributing to the broader economy. Starting

VENTURE INTO A GLOBAL ENTITY

a business offers immigrants a path toward building wealth, creating jobs, and establishing a legacy in their adopted country.

For many immigrants like me, the H1-B visa provided entry into the U.S. workforce through skilled employment, allowing us to contribute our talents to needy industries. The entrepreneurial drive often seen in immigrants, who have already overcome great odds to get here, gives them a unique advantage in the marketplace. Studies show that immigrants frequently outpace native-born citizens in starting businesses because they are more willing to take calculated risks, embrace innovation, and find creative solutions to problems.

Entrepreneurship also enables immigrants to leverage their unique cultural perspectives and networks, which can be particularly useful in food, retail, technology, and services. Drawing on global experiences while navigating the local economy gives immigrant entrepreneurs a distinct edge, allowing them to exceed expectations and build thriving enterprises. By pursuing entrepreneurship, immigrants create opportunities for themselves and enrich the economy and the communities they become a part of.

Global Leadership Insights

1. *Faith as a Pillar in Decision-Making*

Faith plays a vital role in leaders' decision-making process, grounding them with confidence and clarity in uncertain times. Leaders who rely on faith, whether spiritual or rooted in personal values, are more likely to approach challenges with optimism and perseverance. Trusting in a higher purpose or guiding principle strengthens a leader's resolve to make tough decisions while maintaining integrity.

2. *The Power of Family as Emotional Support*

A solid foundation in family relationships often supports strong leadership. Leaders who can rely on their nuclear family for emotional support create a safe space to reflect and recharge. This stability fosters emotional intelligence, an essential trait for leaders facing the pressures of decision-making, conflict resolution, and maintaining a balance between personal and professional life.

3. *Cultural Adaptation Enhances Leadership Versatility*

Leaders who have navigated different cultural contexts, as outlined in the chapter's discussions on adapting to both American and Nigerian cultures, develop a heightened sense of cultural intelligence. This flexibility enables them to engage and lead effectively in diverse environments.

Respecting and balancing various cultural perspectives while staying true to one's roots is valuable in global leadership.

4. *Leveraging Financial Literacy for Strategic Leadership*

Financial independence is crucial for leaders, as it provides the freedom to make decisions without being hindered by monetary constraints. Leaders who invest time in understanding complex economic systems, managing budgets, and making informed investment decisions are better positioned to create sustainable growth. Financial literacy in leadership is about wealth-building and empowering those they lead through sound financial stewardship.

5. *Building Resilience Through Faith in Times of Adversity*

The ability to lead effectively in times of adversity often comes down to resilience. Leaders who cultivate faith, especially during challenging periods, learn to rely on inner strength and divine guidance to navigate tricky situations. This resilience is about enduring hardships and transforming them into personal and professional growth opportunities.

Conclusion

Mentorship plays an undeniable role in the foundation of any meaningful success. Whether through family members who instill our earliest values, educators who open our minds to new possibilities, or professionals who guide our steps into the workforce, mentors are catalysts for growth and learning. Drawing from their wisdom, we also understand our responsibility to guide others.

Our next tackle is the trials and triumphs that arise from facing adversity head-on, exploring how resilience becomes the cornerstone for personal and professional transformation.

CHAPTER 8

THE POWER OF MENTORSHIP

MENTORSHIP IS FUNDAMENTAL in personal and professional development, offering guidance, support, and wisdom from those who have walked a similar path. Mentorship can be particularly transformative for immigrants, bridging unfamiliar terrain and the knowledge needed to thrive in a new environment. A good mentor shares experiences, helps navigate challenges and opens doors to new opportunities, offering a framework for growth that might otherwise be difficult to attain. The mentor-mentee relationship fosters confidence, enhances skill, and encourages continuous learning.

Role Models as Catalysts for Success

Role models are powerful catalysts for success. They inspire and shape our aspirations, behaviors, and goals. They provide real-life examples of what can be achieved through perseverance, discipline, and dedication. Whether it is family members, mentors, or public figures, role models show us what is possible and push us to strive for greater accomplishments.

Their influence helps us define our values and motivates us to pursue paths that align with our potential. Role models are powerful catalysts for success, inspiring and shaping our aspirations, behaviors, and goals. They provide real-life examples of what can be achieved through perseverance, discipline, and dedication.

Whether it is family members, mentors, or public figures, role models show us what is possible and push us to strive for greater accomplishments. Their influence helps us define our values and motivates us to pursue paths that align with our potential. Observing their triumphs and learning from their experiences gives us invaluable insights, which can propel us forward in our undertakings.

Influential Family Members

From the earliest years of my life, my parents were my first and most consistent role models. My father and mother played pivotal roles in shaping the foundation of who I became, not just as an individual but also as a leader. They imparted values rooted in our strong family cultural heritage, a code I have carried into adulthood and beyond.

VENTURE INTO A GLOBAL ENTITY

My father was a man of discipline and structure. He had to navigate his career amidst financial constraints, yet his determination to provide a better future for his children became his driving force. His resilience in the face of adversity demonstrated that authentic leadership begins at home, with the example one sets for one's family.

On the other hand, my mother modeled grace and nurturing, showing me the importance of balancing ambition with empathy. She taught me to appreciate the softer, often overlooked elements of leadership, such as understanding, patience, and the power of emotional support. Together, my parents instilled in me an unshakable sense of duty and a deep respect for our cultural and familial traditions. These early lessons shaped the values I bring into my personal and professional life today.

Mentors in Education

Several teachers left an indelible mark on my life throughout my educational journey. These mentors were more than just educators. They were guides who broadened my understanding of the world and encouraged me to think beyond my immediate circumstances.

My economics teacher helped me realize the importance of financial literacy, a lesson that has played a crucial role in my life's success. Their teachings went beyond textbooks, planting seeds of curiosity and critical thinking that allowed me to view the world from different perspectives.

Similarly, my agricultural and geography teachers inspired me to think holistically about the environment and our place in it. These subjects taught me about the interconnectedness of the world and the importance of understanding one's surroundings, both locally and globally. Their teachings broadened my worldview and helped me see that no matter where you come from, there are always lessons to learn from others.

One of the greatest lessons I learned from these mentors was that education is not just about passing exams or securing a job—it is about gaining wisdom. They reminded me that mistakes are growth opportunities.

Each mentor, in their own way, made me understand that learning from failures is just as important, if not more, than celebrating successes. Through their guidance, I learned to embrace humility, knowing that pursuing knowledge is a lifelong journey.

Professional Mentors

The Holy Book says, "He that walketh with wise men shall be wise: but a companion of fools shall be destroyed." This wisdom has stayed with me throughout my professional career. I have been fortunate to walk with wise mentors who have guided me with their knowledge and experience.

These individuals, from the medical field and beyond, have been instrumental in shaping my professional path. They have taught me that success is not solely about skill or intellect but also about the ability to learn from others and to surround oneself with people who inspire and challenge you.

In my practice, I have encountered mentors who have taught me the technical aspects of my profession and the moral and ethical responsibilities that come with it. They have shown me the importance of empathy in patient care, restoring physical well-being, and the emotional and psychological health of those we serve. Their guidance has made a profound difference in my understanding of what it means to be a true professional who strives for excellence but never loses sight of the humanity behind the work.

These professional mentors helped me navigate the fine line between creating poverty and prosperity for others. They showed me that in any profession, especially in healthcare, the real difference lies in the ability to alleviate pain and restore joy, and that has been one of the most rewarding aspects of my career.

Public Figures and Historical Leaders

Beyond my immediate circle of family, educators, and colleagues, public figures and historical leaders have also significantly shaped my approach to leadership.

Throughout my life, I have been drawn to biographies of individuals who have overcome adversity to achieve greatness. Figures like Nelson Mandela, Mahatma Gandhi, and others who have fought for justice, freedom, and equality have inspired me to think beyond my ambitions and consider how my actions could impact society.

Reading the stories of these leaders has taught me invaluable lessons about resilience, adaptability, and the power of conviction. These individuals did not let their circumstances dictate their future; instead, they used their hardships as steppingstones to more outstanding achievements. Their stories remind me that authentic leadership is about service and leaving a legacy that uplifts others.

What stands out most is that these historical and personal mentors have always been more interested in my future than in my past. They are focused on what I can become rather than what I have already achieved. This mindset has helped me push forward, continually aiming to improve myself and those around me.

They have also helped me see the blind spots that I could not recognize on my own, the weaknesses that, if left unchecked, could hinder my success. This insight has been invaluable in shaping my growth as a leader and person.

Gaining Wisdom and Skills

Gaining wisdom and skills is an ongoing process that enriches personal and professional life. Wisdom is applying knowledge thoughtfully, understanding its deeper implications, and making sound judgments. It comes not only from formal education but also from life experiences, challenges, and reflections. Skill development is about honing specific technical or interpersonal abilities that help us excel in our fields.

Wisdom and skills form the foundation of success, enabling us to adapt, grow, and make informed decisions in various aspects of life. Combining these two elements allows us to navigate complexities confidently, opening doors to new opportunities and personal growth.

Absorbing Knowledge

Wisdom, as the old saying goes, is the principal thing. From a young age, I have always sought to fill my mind with knowledge, understanding that wisdom is the cornerstone of success. Pursuing knowledge has been an integral part of my personal and professional life. I invested heavily in books, taking every opportunity to read and research new topics.

Whether it was a visit to the library or a quiet evening at home, I found solace and growth in the written word. The love for knowledge is one of the driving forces behind my decision to continue my education to the highest levels, achieving professional heights many only dream of.

Books are more than just resources; they are windows into the minds of great thinkers and doers who came before us. Through reading, I have learned lessons that stretch beyond the confines of my immediate experience. This passion for learning has shaped me into a lifelong student, eager to absorb knowledge wherever it is found. Knowledge and wisdom are the foundation for successful careers and fulfilled lives.

Skills Development

While absorbing knowledge is crucial, applying that knowledge is equally important. Skill development has been a cornerstone of my professional growth. From my training in physiotherapy to the numerous certifications I have pursued over the years, I have always sought to expand my skills.

Beyond the structured environments of universities and training programs, I have taken it upon myself to develop my abilities through self-study. My home library is filled with books I use for reference and as tools for my continuous personal development.

Additionally, I have actively pursued various training programs in my field, earning certifications that enhance my expertise. However, it is not just about formal training;

on-the-job experience has also significantly influenced my growth.

I have learned immensely from colleagues and mentors, absorbing and integrating their lessons into my practice. This has made me a better professional and a more well-rounded individual. Learning never stops, and I embrace every opportunity to acquire new skills that elevate my career.

Teachability and Agility

Across my practice in Africa, Europe, and North America, I have always maintained a teachable spirit. I firmly believe that no one ever stops learning and that philosophy has guided my work ethic wherever I go. Whether learning from senior colleagues, peers, or even subordinates, I remain open to gaining new perspectives and insights. Humility in learning has allowed me to gather a wide array of experiences, and each new encounter adds another layer of expertise to my practice.

Mental agility, in addition to being teachable, has been a critical attribute in my career. I have encountered numerous complex problems in my field, and the ability to apply critical thinking has enabled me to navigate these challenges successfully.

I do not shy away from intricate problems; instead, I use them as opportunities to sharpen my problem-solving abilities. Through this combination of teachability and agility, I have thrived in diverse environments and applied my knowledge effectively.

Building Confidence

A growth mindset has been essential in building my confidence, especially when faced with challenging situations. Over the years, I have learned to treat myself respectfully, valuing my strengths and acknowledging my weaknesses without allowing them to hinder my progress. I believe in the power of self-affirmation, constantly reminding myself of the skills I have gained and the progress I have made.

Confidence does not come overnight; it is built over time through experience, learning, and self-awareness. By tracking my progress and setting clear goals, I have been able to grow my confidence and take on increasingly challenging tasks. Whether treating patients with complex conditions or managing projects with high stakes, my self-confidence has guided me to tackle every obstacle head-on.

Mentoring Others

Mentoring others is a rewarding and transformative experience, both for the mentor and the mentee. It involves offering guidance, sharing knowledge, and providing support to help individuals reach their full potential. Through mentoring, we pass down the wisdom gained from our experiences, helping others navigate challenges and achieve their goals.

Mentoring fosters personal growth, strengthens professional networks, and cultivates a spirit of collaboration. It goes beyond imparting knowledge; it inspires confidence, encourages lifelong learning, and creates lasting relationships that empower both parties to continue evolving. As we mentor others, we contribute to a cycle of growth and success that benefits not just individuals but entire communities.

Cross-Cultural Mentoring

Mentoring different cultures has been one of the most fulfilling aspects of my personal and professional journey. As someone who values openness and empathy, I have made it a point to mentor individuals from diverse backgrounds, offering guidance, support, and a safe environment to foster their growth. This extends to my children, as I have raised them to understand the importance of empathy in relationships, regardless of race, gender, ethnicity, religious or cultural background, or sexual orientation.

Cross-cultural mentoring is more than just giving advice; it is about actively listening, understanding different perspectives, and providing a bridge between diverse experiences. I have made it my mission to teach the next generation how to navigate the complexities of our multicultural world with empathy and respect. Mentoring others in this way enriches their lives and broadens my understanding of the human experience, making me more adaptable and open to new ideas.

Mentoring for Career Transition

Career transitions can be daunting, especially when navigating unfamiliar job markets. In my own life, I have gone through multiple transitions, from moving between continents to switching industries. With these experiences in mind, I have mentored many Nigerian therapists who have relocated to the United States, helping them set professional goals, maintain accountability, and tap into valuable networks.

As a mentor, I provide moral support and industrial insight to those going through significant career shifts, helping them adapt and succeed. I guide them in aligning their skills with market demands and building a network of connections to ease their transition. I offer practical advice and emotional and moral support to make all the difference in such a pivotal time. It is a rewarding experience, knowing that my guidance helps others succeed in environments that were once unfamiliar to me.

Mentorship Through Lifelong Learning

Lifelong learning has always been a fundamental principle for me, and I emphasize this in my mentorship. Throughout my life, I have faced personal and professional challenges that have taught me invaluable lessons. I use these experiences to provide constructive feedback to my mentees, helping them navigate their struggles with a clearer perspective.

Mentorship is not just about teaching; it is about inspiring others to continuously pursue knowledge and develop resilience in the face of challenges. I help my mentees set new goals, acquire new skills, and recognize the importance of growth, no matter where they are. By sharing my journey of learning and overcoming obstacles, I show them that no challenge is impossible with the right mindset and effort.

Digital and Remote Mentoring

With the rise of digital communication, I have adapted my mentoring approach to include virtual mentoring. Sharing my life experiences through virtual platforms has allowed me to reach a wider audience, including family members and mentees across continents. Whether through video calls, social media, or online discussions, I provide guidance and support to those who seek my advice.

Digital mentoring allows for more flexibility and accessibility. It allows me to be present for my mentees, regardless of their location. I can share my experiences and wisdom using social media and other online platforms, offering a valuable anchor for those navigating the complexities of life and career. Virtual mentorship has become essential in my mission to help others grow and succeed, proving that distance is no barrier to meaningful guidance.

Pay It Forward

Paying it forward is creating a positive ripple effect that extends beyond ourselves. It involves taking the wisdom, kindness, and opportunities we have received and passing them on to others without expecting anything in return. This practice is rooted in the belief that by helping others, we contribute to a cycle of goodwill that can uplift entire communities and inspire others to do the same.

Paying it forward can take many forms, such as mentoring, sharing resources, or simply offering support to someone in need. It is about recognizing that we are all part of a larger network of human connections and that each act of generosity can ignite change in someone else's life, fostering a culture of compassion and shared success. Here is how you can pay it forward.

Promote the Value of Mentorship

Mentorship has been a driving force in my personal and professional growth, and I have become deeply passionate about sharing my knowledge and experiences with others. The relationships I have built with my mentees bring me immense joy, especially seeing them achieve their milestones and grow. Mentoring allows me to pass down wisdom and is a continuous learning experience.

Each mentoring interaction brings new insights, and I am constantly excited by the prospect of teaching and learning. Celebrating the success of my mentees makes the journey fulfilling as I see them develop into strong, confident individuals who, in turn, have the potential to mentor others.

Create Opportunities for Mentorship

One of the most effective ways to ensure that mentorship thrives is by creating spaces where it can flourish. Networking is crucial in opening doors for these opportunities, as it connects individuals who may benefit from mentoring relationships. I have always believed that solid networks are essential for personal and professional growth, and I strive to foster such connections.

By facilitating introductions and sharing resources, I give my mentees a broader horizon of opportunities that can lead to growth and development. Effective mentorship does not just offer guidance; it also leads to tangible rewards both for the mentor and the mentee, as it fosters a cycle of learning, giving, and receiving.

Encourage Peer Mentorship

While the traditional mentor-mentee dynamic is valuable, I also encourage a more horizontal approach: peer mentorship, where colleagues or friends exchange skills and expertise. This can be incredibly enriching, as it fosters a culture of two-way communication and allows individuals to expose each other to new perspectives and challenge existing ideas.

Peer mentorship helps create an environment where everyone can learn from each other, regardless of rank or experience. It fosters camaraderie and mutual respect, which is essential for a supportive and innovative work or learning environment.

Mentorship as a Legacy

Mentorship is about the present and leaving behind a lasting impact. I often think about my grandfather, whose legacy lives on through the land on which schools were built. Though he passed away long ago, his actions still influence many lives, including mine. In the same way, I aspire to leave a legacy that will endure long after I am gone.

Through my entrepreneurial ventures and philanthropic efforts, I hope to be remembered for what I achieved and how I helped others achieve their dreams. I hold the idea of paying it forward dear, and I aim to build a legacy of giving, mentoring, and inspiring future generations to carry on the torch of self-improvement and community empowerment.

Global Leadership Insights

The Power of Role Models in Leadership

Global leaders often draw inspiration from various role models, whether family members, mentors, or historical figures. These influences provide the moral framework and professional guidance necessary for success, demonstrating the importance of seeking wisdom from those who have gone before us.

Continuous Learning and Skill Development

Effective global leadership requires a commitment to lifelong learning. Absorbing knowledge through formal education, self-study, and practical experiences across different cultural contexts equips leaders with the wisdom and agility to adapt to the ever-changing global landscape.

Mentorship as a Key to Cross-Cultural Leadership

Global leaders thrive by offering and receiving mentorship across diverse cultures. Sharing experiences and building relationships with individuals from different backgrounds fosters empathy and understanding, helping leaders navigate cross-cultural challenges with respect and insight.

Building Confidence Through Adaptability

Confidence in leadership stems from a growth mindset and adaptability. Leaders who embrace critical thinking and mental agility can confront complex problems with poise, continuously learning from their peers and subordinates in various global contexts.

Paying It Forward as a Leadership Legacy

Authentic leadership is about creating a legacy through mentorship. By fostering the growth of others and encouraging peer mentorship, leaders build stronger communities and ensure that their influence endures beyond their careers, touching future generations.

Conclusion

As we come to the close of Part 3, it is evident that the journey across oceans, cultures, and opportunities has not just been about physical relocation but about personal transformation. Moving to new environments has shown how crucial adaptability, resilience, and a deep sense of purpose are to success, not just in one's career but in pursuing a better life.

Building a foundation in a new land has been challenging and triumphant, setting the stage for something greater. These experiences forged through perseverance and courage, have crafted a future without geography or circumstance limiting possibilities.

As we look ahead, the story evolves from personal growth and professional achievement to leadership, where the seeds of experience begin to blossom into broader aspirations. The excursion thus far has been about establishing a foothold, but the next phase invites us to embrace a vision for the future that transcends borders and redefines leadership on a global scale.

With a solid foundation built, it is time to look forward to what lies beyond the horizon. Welcome to Part 4.

DR. OLAJIDE OKUNROUNMU

PART 4

VISIONARY LEADERSHIP AND FUTURE ASPIRATIONS

DR. OLAJIDE OKUNROUNMU

CHAPTER 9

DEFINING VISIONARY LEADERSHIP

VISIONARY LEADERSHIP is often defined by the ability to see beyond the present and imagine a future that others may not yet envision. It requires forward-thinking, the capacity to inspire, the decisiveness to take bold steps, and the empathy to lead with compassion and inclusiveness.

A visionary leader is not just focused on personal success but is driven by the desire to create a legacy that empowers others. In this chapter, we will explore the characteristics that define visionary leadership and how these traits have shaped the author's life and career. From developing a personal vision to leading with integrity, we will examine the core qualities that every visionary leader must cultivate in their journey toward making a lasting impact.

Characteristics of Visionary Leadership

Visionary leadership is about having great ideas and turning those ideas into reality through strategic action. Leaders who possess this ability are forward thinkers who anticipate changes and adapt quickly. They inspire and motivate others, make decisive choices even in uncertain times, and foster inclusivity and empathy in their leadership approach. These characteristics allow visionary leaders to not only build successful careers but also to make a meaningful difference in the lives of others.

Forward Thinking

Since childhood, I have envisioned a future where I can significantly impact those who are disadvantaged. This unique ability to imagine and plan for a better future has guided me through personal and professional endeavors. From my early years, I have been able to project where my industries are heading, embracing shifts in consumer needs and technological advances to stay ahead. This forward-thinking mindset has been instrumental in shaping my approach to leadership, enabling me to seize opportunities before they arise.

A visionary leader's ability to look ahead and anticipate future trends is a fundamental trait. Forward-thinking leaders predict changes in their environment and create strategies to adapt to and leverage them. This characteristic goes beyond personal success—it is about shaping the future for others, especially in a rapidly evolving world.

Visionary leaders often study global trends, technological advancements, and emerging markets to stay ahead. They are flexible, adaptable, and unafraid to pivot when needed, always positioning themselves to seize new opportunities. In a world increasingly driven by innovation, forward-thinking leaders empower others by preparing them for the future and cultivating resilience and adaptability within their teams.

Inspirational and Motivation

My upbringing, rooted deeply in family values and religious beliefs, has always been a source of strength and inspiration for me. This foundation has equipped me with a compelling vision that I use to motivate others. Whether through risk-taking, resilience, or my passion for growth and innovation, I have always believed in leading by example. I have learned to inspire those around me, encouraging them to strive for greatness and remain focused on achieving their goals, no matter how challenging the path is.

While personal inspiration and motivation can come from one's upbringing or religious background, a visionary leader inspires others. They embody the values they wish to instill in their followers and model behaviors that ignite passion and drive. Inspirational leaders do not just tell others what to do. They show them what is possible by overcoming their challenges and leading authentically.

Additionally, visionary leaders foster environments where others feel safe to express their ideas, take risks, and grow. They challenge conventional thinking, encourage creativity, and push their teams toward continuous improvement. This ripple effect of inspiration leads to a motivated, dynamic workforce eager to pursue shared goals.

Decisive and Confident

Leadership demands bold decisions, especially when navigating uncharted waters. I chose to pursue a career in physiotherapy, an unknown profession at the time, despite societal expectations to follow more traditional paths like medicine, law, or engineering. Similarly, moving to the U.S. without any close family members as guides required bold decision-making.

I confidently faced the unknown, understanding that visionary leaders must often face uncertainty with determination. These experiences have shaped my ability to make tough decisions and face challenges head-on, qualities that have been crucial in overcoming setbacks and propelling me forward.

Decisiveness is essential in leadership because indecision can stall progress and breed uncertainty. However, confident leaders do not make decisions in isolation; they are skilled in gathering relevant information, consulting experts, and weighing the potential risks and benefits before acting. Once a decision is made, they commit fully and take responsibility for the outcomes.

It also involves the ability to course-correct when necessary. Confident leaders are not afraid to admit mistakes and take corrective action. This quality builds trust among team members, as they know their leader will make bold decisions in the face of uncertainty while also being accountable for the results. Confidence in leadership is contagious, empowering others to trust their judgment and act decisively.

Empathetic and Inclusive

One key trait of a visionary leader is empathy. I have always believed in seeing things from others' perspectives, which has allowed me to build inclusive teams and strong relationships. Whether in my business dealings or personal interactions, I remain committed to being transparent and honest.

Leaders should inspire, listen to, and learn from those they lead, fostering an environment where everyone's voice matters. This inclusive approach has been at the core of my leadership style, helping me build a cohesive team and inspire others to realize their potential.

Empathy in leadership creates stronger connections with people, making visionary leaders more effective. By understanding the emotions, perspectives, and challenges of others, empathetic leaders are better equipped to create inclusive environments where everyone feels valued. This inclusivity goes beyond simply listening. It involves actively seeking input from diverse voices and ensuring all team members have the resources and support they need to succeed.

Empathetic leaders also recognize the importance of emotional intelligence in handling conflicts, addressing concerns, and fostering collaboration. Empathy allows leaders to unify teams and communities, guiding them toward common goals in a globalized world where diversity of thought and background is more crucial than ever. Moreover, inclusive leaders inspire loyalty and commitment, as individuals are likelier to invest in a vision when they feel understood and appreciated.

Developing a Personal Vision

Developing a personal vision requires deep self-reflection and clarity. It is about seeing beyond the immediate challenges and distractions and focusing on a future aligned with your values, passions, and goals. A well-defined personal vision is a guiding compass, helping you make decisions, overcome setbacks, and stay motivated throughout your leadership.

Whether in business, community, or personal life, creating a vision empowers you to turn possibilities into realities, ensuring that each step leads to meaningful progress. The following subchapters reveal key aspects of developing this vision, from self-reflection to aligning actions with purpose.

Self-Reflections and Clarity

Self-reflection is consciously examining one's thoughts, actions, emotions, and motives. Leadership involves taking a step back to assess one's strengths, weaknesses, decision-making processes, and overall leadership style. This introspection allows leaders to understand better their behavior, how it affects others, and where improvement is needed.

I have always believed in taking the time to reflect on the bigger picture and seeing myself as blessed to be a blessing to others. Whether adapting to diverse cultures or facing new challenges, I constantly seek clarity in my purpose. Each day, I make it a point to learn something new, whether from social media, reading books, or interacting with others. This commitment to self-reflection allows me to stay grounded in my values while remaining open to new possibilities.

Self-reflection promotes awareness of personal biases, blind spots, and areas that require development, creating an environment of continuous learning and personal growth. Through regular self-reflection, leaders can enhance their decision-making abilities, align their actions with their core values, and ensure that their vision remains clear and focused. This clarity also helps leaders communicate their goals and expectations more effectively to their teams, fostering trust, motivation, and a stronger sense of direction.

Incorporating mindfulness and journaling into daily routines can significantly enhance self-reflection. Regularly documenting thoughts, feelings, and observations helps leaders track their progress, identify recurring patterns, and adjust their goals accordingly. Mindfulness practices, such as meditation, help cultivate presence and self-awareness, allowing leaders to remain grounded in their vision even during turbulent times.

Set Realistic Goals

Setting realistic goals as a leader means defining clear, achievable objectives that align with both the leader's vision and the organization's capacity to accomplish them. Realistic goals are not only specific and attainable but also consider the available resources, time limits, and potential obstacles that may arise while pursuing those goals. It involves balancing ambition with practicality, ensuring that while the goals are challenging, they remain within reach given the current conditions and context.

As a visionary leader, not only dream big but use the SMART framework to set achievable goals:
- Specific
- Measurable
- Achievable
- Relevant and
- Time-based

I use them to guide my short and long-term objectives. Whether expanding my business or creating new opportunities for others, I ensure that every goal is grounded, ensuring that the steps I take today will lead to success tomorrow.

For leaders, setting realistic goals also includes considering their team's skills and strengths and ensuring that the goals push the team toward growth without overwhelming them. This approach promotes motivation and sustained progress because the team feels empowered to meet objectives rather than discouraged by targets too far out of reach. Leaders who set realistic goals clearly understand their organization's capabilities, the market environment, and team members' personal and professional limits.

Craft a Vision Statement:

A vision is a clear and compelling picture of the future that an individual, organization, or leader aspires to achieve. It reflects long-term aspirations, goals, and the desired impact, serving as a guiding star that inspires and directs actions. In leadership, a vision articulates what success looks like in the future, the values that will drive the organization, and the purpose that motivates everyone involved. A well-crafted vision provides a sense of purpose and a roadmap for decision-making and strategic planning.

Our vision is to deliver unparalleled excellence across our core businesses, including real estate, healthcare services, nursing and rehabilitation care, and financial services. We aim to empower individuals and communities by providing innovative financing solutions, investments, and advertising strategies that foster long-term growth and stability. Through our commitment to quality and compassion, we strive to make a lasting impact on those we serve and drive positive change in the industries we operate in.

How a Leader Can Craft a Vision:

Reflect on Core Values and Purpose: A vision starts with understanding what deeply matters to the leader and the organization. Reflecting on core values helps define the guiding principles shaping the vision. Leaders should ask themselves and their team: *Why do we do what we do? What impact do we want?* Clarifying this purpose grounds the vision in meaningful and inspiring ideals.

Understand the Big Picture: Crafting a vision requires a leader to think beyond the immediate tasks and look at the larger context, including market trends, societal needs, and future possibilities. A leader must consider their organization's broader landscape and anticipate how it may evolve. This helps the leader shape a vision that is both aspirational and relevant.

Engage Stakeholders: A powerful vision resonates with all those involved in its realization. Leaders should engage with key stakeholders, team members, clients, customers, and the community to gather insights on their needs, expectations, and hopes for the future. This engagement fosters shared ownership, ensures an inclusive vision, and reflects diverse perspectives.

Set Ambitious Yet Realistic Goals: A vision should be ambitious, pushing the organization beyond its current state, but must also be grounded. Crafting a vision means striking a balance between inspiration and practicality. Given the organization's resources and capabilities, leaders should aim for something exciting and challenging yet achievable within a reasonable timeframe.

Make It Clear and Memorable: A vision must be concise, compelling, and easy to communicate. A leader should avoid jargon and focus on clarity, using inspiring and straightforward language. A memorable vision energizes the team, guiding day-to-day actions while considering the long-term future.

Align Actions with the Vision: Once the vision is crafted, it must inform every aspect of leadership and decision-making. The leader must continuously align the organization's strategies, goals, and actions with the vision. This ensures consistent efforts and motivates individuals to work collectively towards the common future.

Example:

A vision could be *"To be the leading provider of sustainable energy solutions, empowering communities and businesses to thrive in a cleaner, greener world."*

Aligning Actions with Visions

Aligning actions with visions means ensuring that every decision, goal, and activity within an organization or leadership practice is directed toward achieving the larger, long-term vision. It involves a leader consistently checking that their strategies, operations, and daily tasks are in harmony with the broader goals and future aspirations they have set out. In practical terms, short-term actions and decisions are not taken in isolation but are guided by how they contribute to the vision.

My vision is clear: to provide superior services in real estate, healthcare, financing, and more while giving back to the community. Through my various business ventures, I aim to create a positive impact beyond financial success. A portion of all profits from my business is dedicated to the Okunrounmu Foundation, which supports underprivileged members of society. This commitment to making a difference drives everything I do, ensuring my vision is personal and communal.

Every action aligns with my broader vision of celebrating success and culture and giving back. By fostering a culture of excellence and inclusivity, I strive to create an environment where people are empowered to reach their full potential. My commitment to giving back is not just a goal but a practice as I continue to invest in the communities that have supported my journey, ensuring that success is shared and multiplied.

Aligning actions with a leader's vision requires ongoing communication, consistent progress monitoring, and a willingness to adapt when necessary. It ensures that every step moves the organization or team closer to fulfilling the desired outcome to generate some of the benefits below.

Benefits to the Leader:

Clarity of Purpose: By aligning actions with a vision, leaders have a clear focus on what needs to be achieved. This clarity helps them make decisions more confidently, knowing that each action serves a bigger purpose. It also reduces distractions and keeps them from veering off course with irrelevant tasks.

Increased Credibility: Leaders who align their actions with their vision demonstrate consistency and integrity. This builds trust and credibility among their team, stakeholders, and external partners, as people see that the leader "walks the talk" and follows through on their promises.

Enhanced Decision-Making: Leaders with a vision to guide their decisions can more easily prioritize and choose actions with the greatest impact. This simplifies decision-making because every choice is measured against whether it supports the long-term vision.

Personal Fulfillment: Leaders who see their vision gradually becoming reality experience a sense of fulfillment and purpose. This helps them stay motivated, even when facing challenges because they can see the bigger picture and the long-term rewards of their efforts.

Benefits to the Organization or People They Lead:

Unified Direction: When leaders align actions with their vision, the organization or team has a clear and unified direction. Employees understand how their work fits the bigger picture and are motivated to contribute to common goals. This unity of purpose fosters collaboration and reduces conflicts arising from misaligned priorities.

Increased Motivation and Engagement: People are more likely to be motivated and engaged when they understand the "why" behind their tasks. Knowing how their work contributes to a larger, inspiring vision gives meaning to everyday tasks and increases their sense of ownership and commitment.

Improved Efficiency: Aligning actions with a vision helps an organization or team use resources more effectively. Time, energy, and finances are allocated to projects that advance the vision, preventing wasted efforts on initiatives that do not serve the long-term goals.

Better Adaptability: When everyone in an organization understands the vision, they can adapt more easily to changes or challenges. Even if unexpected events occur, the team can quickly realign and find ways to stay on track toward the vision. This flexibility is key to long-term success.

Sustainable Growth: An organization builds momentum and achieves steady, sustainable growth by aligning actions with a vision. Rather than focusing on short-term gains that might be unsustainable, the focus on the vision ensures that growth is strategic, meaningful, and lasting.

Example:

A company whose vision is to "become the leading provider of innovative healthcare solutions" will ensure that its product development, marketing strategies, and customer service efforts all contribute to this goal. Every department knows its role is to innovate, improve healthcare outcomes, and lead the market in this domain, creating synergy across the organization.

In summary, aligning actions with visions ensures that every step taken is intentional and productive and contributes to long-term success for leaders and those they lead. It cultivates focus, credibility, and sustained progress, empowering organizations and teams to achieve meaningful results.

Leading With Integrity and Authenticity

Integrity is the unwavering commitment to ethical principles. Leaders with integrity do not just set rules. They live by them, creating a culture where honesty, fairness, and accountability thrive. This means making decisions that are beneficial in the short term and aligned with moral and ethical standards in the long term.

For example, a leader with integrity might face a situation where cutting corners could bring immediate profit or success. Still, they uphold the organization's values and do things correctly, even if it takes longer or costs more. This demonstrates a deep commitment to doing what is right rather than easy.

Integrity also involves owning mistakes. A leader who is quick to admit they are wrong fosters an environment of openness, where team members feel safe to take risks, knowing that learning from failure is part of the journey. It promotes accountability throughout the organization, encouraging others to act with the same level of honesty.

Authentic leadership means being real and transparent about who you are, your strengths, and your weaknesses. It is about leading without pretense, not trying to project an image of perfection but allowing people to see your true self. Authentic leaders build stronger connections because people are drawn to their sincerity.

An authentic leader does not try to imitate others or follow trends just for approval. Instead, they live in a way that reflects their genuine personality and beliefs. This makes their leadership more relatable and sustainable because they are not forcing themselves into a role that does not fit. By being authentic, leaders show vulnerability and humanity, making them more approachable and easier to trust.

For example, an authentic leader might openly communicate their uncertainties during challenging times, inviting the team to share ideas and contribute to solutions. This does not diminish their authority; it creates a collaborative environment where everyone feels valued and empowered.

Integrity and authenticity are non-negotiable qualities for any visionary leader. True leadership is more than achieving personal success; it is about setting an example through honest, transparent, and ethical behavior. Authentic leaders inspire trust, and their credibility is built on consistency between their words and actions. Integrity and authenticity have been central to my leadership style.

Defining personal ethics:

The core values of honesty, compassion, self-respect, and fairness guide my leadership and have shaped my approach to personal and professional relationships. Maintaining high ethical standards, whether in small or significant matters, is essential to earning the trust of those around me.

Components of Defining Personal Ethics:

Core Values: Core values are the fundamental beliefs that shape a person's worldview and actions. These values include honesty, fairness, respect, kindness, accountability, and loyalty. When individuals define their ethics, they reflect on which values matter most to them and how they want these values to guide their behavior.

Moral Responsibility: Personal ethics also involve recognizing moral responsibilities and obligations to others and society. This includes treating people with respect, acting with fairness, and ensuring one's actions contribute positively to the well-being of others.

Integrity: Integrity is a key aspect of personal ethics. It means being honest and consistent in one's actions, even when no one is watching. For leaders, integrity ensures that decisions are made transparently and ethically, without compromise.

Accountability: Personal ethics require taking responsibility for one's actions. Leaders who define and adhere to their ethics are willing to own their mistakes and make amends when necessary. Accountability fosters trust and credibility.

Impact of Defining Personal Ethics for Leaders

Consistency in Decision-Making: Well-defined personal ethics help leaders remain consistent. Rather than being swayed by short-term gains or external pressures, leaders with a strong ethical foundation stay true to their principles, ensuring that their actions align with their core beliefs.

Building Trust: Leaders acting according to their ethics build trust with their teams, stakeholders, and clients. People trust those who are transparent, honest, and fair in their dealings. This trust forms the foundation of strong relationships within an organization.

Creating an Ethical Culture: When leaders define their ethics and consistently demonstrate those values, they set the tone for the organization. Employees are more likely to act ethically if they see their leader leading by example. This creates an ethical workplace culture where integrity and fairness are prioritized.

Guiding Through Difficult Situations: Personal ethics serve as a guide during tough decisions. Leaders face complex challenges, and having a clear ethical framework helps them navigate these situations without compromising their integrity. For example, leaders may have to make choices that impact profit, people, or social responsibilities. Defining personal ethics ensures that these decisions are made with a moral foundation.

Enhanced Leadership Effectiveness: Leaders who clearly define their ethics often have a stronger sense of purpose and direction. External pressures or conflicts do not easily sway them because they are grounded in their principles. This enhances their effectiveness as leaders and helps them inspire others.

How to define personal ethics:

Self-Reflection: The process starts with deep self-reflection, where individuals evaluate their life experiences, beliefs, and the values they hold dear. This includes thinking about what they stand for and what kind of leader they want to be.

Clarifying Values: Individuals must identify the values that are most important to them. These might include fairness, compassion, respect, honesty, and accountability. The goal is to ensure these values are actionable, not just abstract ideals.

Establishing Ethical Boundaries: Defining personal ethics also involves setting boundaries for behavior. This means understanding what actions are non-negotiable and aligning behavior with those boundaries in all situations, even when faced with difficult choices.

Communicating Ethics: Once personal ethics are defined, it is important to communicate these values to others, especially in leadership roles. Leading by example and being vocal about ethical principles reinforces the commitment to living and leading by those values.

Defining personal ethics involves understanding one's moral values and using them as a foundation for behavior and decision-making. For leaders, having a clear ethical framework builds trust, ensures consistency in actions, and helps create an ethical culture within organizations, leading to long-term success.

Authentic Communication:

Authentic communication goes beyond simply exchanging information. It is about conveying your message with honesty, openness, and a genuine commitment to transparency. For a leader, this means telling people what they want and need to hear, whether the news is good or bad. Authentic communication builds bridges between leaders and their teams by fostering trust and respect.

Being genuine and transparent is crucial in any relationship. I strive to show my true self, flaws and all, in every interaction, ensuring that the people I work with know they can count on me to be honest and understanding. Authentic communication creates a foundation of trust and allows for more meaningful connections.

When transparent, leaders allow the people they lead to see their true selves, motivations, values, and intentions. This openness invites the same honesty from others, creating a culture where individuals feel safe expressing their opinions and concerns without fear of judgment.

Authentic communication is a two-way street, where listening is just as important as speaking. Leaders who communicate authentically listen attentively and respond thoughtfully, valuing the input of their team members.

Another key element of authentic communication is consistency. When leaders communicate authentically, their words and actions align, helping maintain credibility. It is one thing to talk about values like integrity or fairness, but when a leader consistently embodies those values through their behavior, the trust within their team deepens.

Authentic communication is not about perfection; it is about being real. Leaders who are comfortable admitting their mistakes or uncertainties show that they, too, are learning and growing alongside their teams. This vulnerability can be a powerful bonding force, encouraging others to be open and genuine.

In the long term, authentic communication strengthens relationships within an organization. It promotes collaboration, as individuals feel heard and respected. It reduces misunderstandings since people are more likely to ask for clarification when they trust their leader will not react defensively. Leaders who embrace authentic communication create environments where innovation thrives, teams are more resilient, and everyone feels empowered to contribute to the collective success.

Building Trust and Credibility:

Building trust and credibility as a leader is foundational to successful leadership. Trust and credibility form the backbone of effective leadership, enabling leaders to inspire and motivate those they lead.

Trust is earned through actions, not words. I work hard to demonstrate that I am knowledgeable, skilled, and committed to excellence in everything I do. Whether in business or community service, I strive to build a reputation of integrity that will stand the test of time, ensuring that future generations will remember me for my values and principles.

For a leader, building trust starts with integrity and doing what they say they will do. When leaders consistently follow through on commitments, big or small, they create a dependable reputation. People are likelier to trust a leader who keeps their promises, even in challenging situations. A transparent leader about their decisions, motivations, and challenges also fosters trust because it shows they have nothing to hide and are willing to share the journey with their team.

Conversely, credibility is established by demonstrating expertise and competence in the leader's field. It is not enough to occupy a leadership position; leaders must consistently show they have the knowledge and skills to guide their team toward success. Leaders who continue learning, stay updated with industry trends and demonstrate a commitment to personal growth reinforce their credibility. They also gain credibility by acknowledging their limitations and seeking help when necessary, showing that they prioritize the team's goals over personal pride.

Leaders also build trust and credibility through their behavior toward others. A leader who treats everyone fairly and respects them, regardless of rank or role, earns the loyalty of those they lead. People are more likely to follow a leader who values their contributions and listens to their concerns. This respect extends to being open to feedback and willing to adjust course when needed, showing that the leader values collaboration and continuous improvement.

Walking the Talk

Walking the talk means that a leader's actions align with their words, reflecting consistency, integrity, and commitment to their values. It is the practical embodiment of leadership by example, where leaders demonstrate the principles and standards they advocate through behavior. For a leader, walking the talk is essential in fostering trust and credibility, as it shows that they do not expect others to do what they are unwilling to do themselves.

I believe in the scripture, "As a man thinks in his heart, so is he." I aim to live out the values I preach, ensuring that my actions align with my words. My goal is to prosper financially and through the spiritual and moral wealth that comes from helping others and positively impacting the world around me.

Leaders who walk the talk set the tone for their organization or group. For instance, if a leader emphasizes the importance of punctuality but they are habitually late, their credibility diminishes. On the other hand, a leader who values hard work and consistently puts in the effort demonstrates their commitment to the shared goals, inspiring others to follow suit. Walking the talk eliminates the perception of hypocrisy, reinforcing that the leader is part of the team and invested in its success.

One key benefit of walking the talk is the ripple effect it creates. When people see their leader practicing what they preach, they are likelier to adopt similar behaviors. It strengthens a culture of accountability, where everyone holds themselves and others to the same standards. For instance, if a leader values open communication and regularly seeks feedback, their team will feel encouraged to communicate more freely, knowing their input is genuinely valued.

Moreover, walking the talk during difficult times when it's hard to do so shows true leadership strength. When leaders uphold their values even when faced with adversity or the temptation to cut corners, it reinforces their integrity and deepens their team's trust. It shows that the leader's principles are not negotiable and are deeply ingrained in their decision-making process.

Walking the talk is about more than just leading by example. It is about creating an environment where actions speak louder than words, and the leader's behavior reminds them of the organization's mission, values, and vision. Leaders who consistently walk the talk foster a culture of integrity, motivation, and shared accountability, driving individual and collective success.

Benefits of Leading with Integrity and Authenticity

Building Stronger Trust: When leaders act with integrity and authenticity, they create a culture of trust within their teams. People are more likely to follow someone they believe is honest, ethical, and true to themselves. Trust is the cornerstone of any successful organization, fostering loyalty, cooperation, and open communication.

Creating a Healthy Organizational Culture: Leaders prioritizing integrity set a standard for the organization. Their commitment to fairness and transparency trickles down to every level, encouraging employees to uphold high ethical standards. This creates a positive, healthy environment where people feel respected and safe.

Enhancing Team Morale: Authentic leaders inspire teams by showing that they are not perfect but are willing to grow and learn alongside them. This humility boosts morale and encourages others to bring their authentic selves to work. When team members feel they can be themselves, they are more engaged and productive.

Encouraging Open Communication: Integrity and authenticity promote honest communication. Leaders who embody these traits are more likely to foster an environment where feedback flows freely, both up and down the hierarchy. People feel safe voicing their concerns, offering suggestions, and challenging ideas because they know their leader values openness.

Sustainable Success: While leaders who lack integrity may find short-term success through manipulation or deception, this is never sustainable. Over time, dishonesty erodes trust, leading to organizational instability. In contrast, leaders who practice integrity and authenticity lay a foundation for long-term success built on strong relationships, consistency, and a positive reputation.

Empowering Others: By being true to themselves and demonstrating integrity, leaders encourage others to do the same. When employees see that their leader values honesty and authenticity, they feel empowered to make decisions based on their values without fear of retribution. This environment encourages innovation and creativity because people can think and act independently.

Challenges of Leading with Integrity and Authenticity:

While leading with integrity and authenticity is rewarding, it has challenges. Sometimes, sticking to one's values means making unpopular decisions or taking the more difficult path. For example, a leader may need to stand against unethical practices within their industry or say no to lucrative deals that do not align with the company's principles. This can sometimes be isolating, but it builds a reputation of trustworthiness and respect in the long run.

Another challenge is that authenticity does not mean complacency. Authenticity requires self-awareness and a willingness to grow. Leaders must balance staying true to their principles with being open to feedback and adapting when necessary. Authenticity is not about stubbornly holding on to one's ways but about being open to evolving while remaining true to core values.

Leading with integrity and authenticity creates a powerful, trust-based leadership style that fosters loyalty, collaboration, and sustainable growth. It sets the stage for a healthy organizational culture and empowers individuals to be their best selves. Leaders who commit to these principles achieve personal success and create a lasting positive impact on those they lead and the organization.

Balancing Personal and Professional Growth

Every leader faces the challenge of balancing personal and professional growth. It requires discipline, time management, and prioritizing tasks without neglecting one's well-being. Leaders must invest in their development while maintaining a healthy work-life balance. Here is how you can approach achieving this balance:

Time Management and Prioritization

Time management and prioritization are essential for any leader aiming to balance personal and professional growth. Effective time management allows a leader to focus on what truly matters, ensuring that the most critical tasks are addressed first while minimizing distractions. Prioritization involves discerning between urgent and important matters and recognizing that not all tasks carry the same weight. For leaders, this means delegating fewer tasks, setting clear goals, and focusing on high-impact activities that align with their vision.

Successful leadership starts with time management. I have learned to prioritize important tasks and remain focused until completion. Flexibility is also key. I adapt quickly to unexpected events while maintaining a clear schedule to meet personal and professional goals.

This could involve organizing the day with set routines and allowing flexibility when unexpected challenges arise. A well-prioritized schedule empowers leaders to balance meeting professional deadlines and caring for their well-being, such as spending time with family or engaging in activities that recharge their energy. In doing so, they increase their productivity and inspire those around them to adopt similar habits.

When leaders manage time effectively and prioritize wisely, they model discipline and purpose, creating a ripple effect within their organization. It helps teams stay focused, reduces stress, and improves outcomes in achieving organizational goals and fostering a healthy work-life balance.

Self-Care and Well-Being

Self-care and well-being are crucial for leaders who want to maintain long-term effectiveness and resilience. A leader's capacity to make sound decisions, inspire others, and navigate challenges often hinges on their mental, physical, and emotional health. By prioritizing self-care, leaders ensure they have the energy and clarity to meet personal and professional demands.

Maintaining mental and physical health is essential in balancing leadership responsibilities. I practice self-care through relaxation, exercise, and prayer, ensuring I manage stress and maintain a positive outlook. Even in a culture that encourages overworking, I prioritize activities that bring me joy and peace, which helps me stay centered in facing challenges.

Engaging in activities that reduce stress, such as regular exercise, meditation, or hobbies, plays a significant role in maintaining balance. Additionally, paying attention to nutrition, sleep, and personal relaxation helps leaders to recharge and stay sharp. It is about creating routines that replenish the body and mind, making it easier to cope with the pressures of leadership.

I get my daily exercise by providing exercises for my patients, boosting my sleeping, eating nutritious food, and engaging in activities that bring personal joy, peace, and happiness.

A leader who practices self-care not only sets a positive example for their team but also cultivates an environment where the well-being of everyone is valued. In doing so, they foster a culture of productivity and engagement while ensuring they remain strong and steady through life's challenges.

Personal Development Planning

Personal development planning is essential for leaders who aim to grow and refine their skills continuously. It involves setting clear, actionable goals for self-improvement and aligning them with personal aspirations and the organization's broader vision. Leaders engaging in personal development planning actively seek learning opportunities through formal education, mentorship, or hands-on experience.

Continuous learning is crucial for growth. I plan to improve my managerial and leadership skills through ongoing education and training. Setting SMART goals keeps me focused on my personal and professional development (OKUNS Brand), ensuring I continue to evolve as a leader.

This process begins with self-assessment, where a leader reflects on their strengths, weaknesses, and areas for growth. Identifying these areas can set specific goals, such as improving communication skills, deepening their expertise in a particular field, or developing emotional intelligence. A well-thought-out plan includes timelines and milestones to track progress and ensure accountability.

The benefits of personal development planning are profound. It keeps leaders adaptable and forward-thinking in a constantly evolving world. Furthermore, leaders who prioritize their growth are better equipped to inspire and support their teams as they model the importance of lifelong learning and self-improvement. This planning enhances their capabilities and strengthens the organization, as an empowered leader can drive innovation and foster a culture of continuous improvement.

Networking and Forming Relationships

Networking and forming relationships are the lifeblood of effective leadership. For any leader, the connections they build and nurture play a vital role in both personal growth and the success of their organization. Building a strong network starts with a genuine interest in others, establishing trust, and sharing common goals or values. These relationships are not just about what you can gain and what you can offer to others; they create a reciprocal bond that enhances collaboration.

I aim to continually build networks within my family, friends, and professional circles by cultivating deep trust and mutual respect based on shared values and interests. Social media platforms like Facebook, LinkedIn, TikTok, and Twitter will be valuable tools in expanding these connections. Additionally, I will strengthen my respect for others in the workplace and my religious community by fostering mutual trust and understanding, regardless of cultural or ethnic differences.

Networking is not confined to the boundaries of traditional meetings or conferences. Leaders today can leverage social media platforms like LinkedIn, Facebook, and even newer ones like TikTok, where they can build relationships across industries and geographic boundaries. The digital age has expanded the reach of networking, allowing leaders to form connections with people they might never have met otherwise.

At its heart, effective networking requires consistent effort and a genuine desire to form lasting connections. It involves taking the time to understand others' goals, challenges, and aspirations while offering support when needed. In the workplace, fostering these relationships is crucial for team cohesion, as it breaks down barriers, builds trust, and opens the doors for more authentic collaboration. Similarly, within your circles, maintaining strong relationships fosters a sense of community and emotional support.

Global Leadership Insights

The Power of Vision to Propel Change

At the heart of any effective leader is envisioning a future that does not yet exist. Leaders with vision inspire others by showing them what could be and guiding them on how to get there. They think beyond today's obstacles, shaping industries and communities with ideas that stretch beyond the current horizon. Global leaders who harness this ability can create movements that inspire innovation and growth, reshaping the future.

Learning from Bold Decisions

True leadership is often about making tough calls, especially when the outcome is uncertain. Visionary leaders do not shy away from risks. They confidently embrace them. The bold decision to pursue the unknown, whether launching a new venture or entering an unfamiliar market, showcases the courage that defines leadership on a global stage. These defining moments push boundaries, spark innovation, and set leaders apart.

Empathy as a Tool for Global Connection

Empathy is not just a soft skill in today's interconnected world; it is imperative for leadership. Visionary leaders build bridges between cultures, understanding that inclusivity is key to collaboration and long-term success. Seeing the world through others' eyes fosters environments where diverse teams thrive and innovation flourishes through collective efforts.

The Role of Integrity in Earning Trust

Trust is the foundation of any successful leadership. Visionary leaders inspire people with ideas and earn their trust by consistently living those values. They walk the talk, whether by demonstrating personal ethics or ensuring transparency in their decisions. This integrity builds credibility, allowing them to lead with authority and respect on a global scale.

Bringing Vision to Life Through Action

A leader's vision is only as good as the actions that support it. Successful global leaders ensure that their strategies, goals, and day-to-day decisions align with their larger vision. This consistency creates a ripple effect, leading teams, organizations, and communities to work purposefully, knowing they are contributing to something greater than themselves.

Conclusion

It has become clear that global success begins with personal vision but flourishes through authenticity, integrity, and growth. True leaders craft their paths clearly and inspire others to walk alongside them. The characteristics we have explored in this chapter, forward-thinking, integrity, and personal balance, form the foundation for leadership that guides and uplifts those around us.

Next, we will see how these principles take root in exemplary leadership, where integrity meets action, and real-life examples like my parents demonstrate the lasting power of leading with heart and principles. Through their stories and the lessons learned from their unwavering dedication, we explore how exemplary leadership is not just defined by traits but by the impact one leaves on others and the legacy of trust and resilience.

CHAPTER 10

EXEMPLARY LEADERSHIP

EXEMPLARY LEADERSHIP IS about more than just guiding others. It is about setting a standard of integrity, dedication, and commitment to excellence that others aspire to follow. Great leaders do not just manage; they inspire. They set the tone for how others engage with their work and how they contribute to something larger than themselves.

Leaders can balance professional success with a deep commitment to integrity and personal growth by reflecting on the examples set by family, personal mentors, and other influences. These qualities resonate in every sphere of leadership, whether in business, community, or family life.

My Parents' Example

The foundations of exemplary leadership are often formed in childhood, shaped by the values and practices observed in the home. For many leaders, parental influence plays a significant role in how they approach their personal and professional lives. My parents' example was no different. They were not just figures of authority; they were role models of hard work, perseverance, and unwavering dedication. Their everyday actions, discipline, and commitment to family shaped my understanding of leading with purpose.

My father, in particular, embodied responsibility. He believed that success resulted from consistent effort and taught me that every small task mattered. Whether it was something as routine as caring for the family or as significant as making life-changing decisions, his approach remained steady, careful, and with integrity. My mother complimented this with her nurturing strength. She balanced the challenges of managing a large family with the grace of someone who understood that true leadership requires empathy as much as authority.

Through their example, I learned that leadership is not confined to the public sphere. True leadership starts at home. It is how you treat your family, balance personal responsibility with care for others, and handle adversity without compromising your values. These early lessons from my parents became the blueprint for how I approach every leadership role I have undertaken, whether in business or community service.

Hardworking and Dedication

Hard work and dedication are fundamental traits of visionary leadership. Leaders who exemplify these qualities understand that achieving great things requires consistent effort, perseverance, and a willingness to go beyond the bare minimum. Hard work isn't just about putting in long hours; it's about working purposefully, staying focused on goals, and continuously improving. Dedication means committing to the vision, even when faced with setbacks, challenges, or obstacles.

My dad led by setting personal examples for others to follow. When his father suffered a stroke while working on his farm and could no longer walk, my dad took two years off his job at UACN's G.B. Ollivant division to care for him. As the firstborn and only son of his mother, he faced great challenges during this time, relying on farm products to survive while caring for his ailing father until his passing two years later. Despite these hardships, my father always shared his life story and struggles with us, his children.

This period also contributed to his inability to further his education beyond the Standard 6 academic level, forcing him to climb the professional ladder from the bottom. Yet, through it all, he demonstrated genuine concern and care for others, taking initiative and personal risks. His leadership style was shared vision, challenging processes, and leading by example, which encouraged and inspired others to do the same. His actions have been a model for me, shaping my approach to leadership and inspiring me to set clear visions and goals, always guided by empathy and perseverance.

A leader's dedication inspires those around them. When leaders are committed to their vision and consistently work hard to bring it to life, it sets the tone for their team or organization. It fosters a culture where others are encouraged to follow suit, knowing their leader is fully invested in their shared goals. Hard work and dedication in leadership are infectious. They create an environment where effort is valued, and no task is too small if it leads to the bigger picture. These qualities become the bedrock upon which trust, respect, and success are built.

Honesty and Transparency

Honesty and transparency are cornerstones of effective and visionary leadership. Leaders who embrace these values foster trust and openness within their teams or organizations. Honesty goes beyond merely telling the truth; it involves being upfront about intentions, limitations, and challenges and acknowledging successes and failures. An honest leader creates a foundation for strong relationships, as people are more inclined to follow someone they believe is authentic and trustworthy.

I strive to align my words with my actions, ensuring I communicate openly and build trust with those I encounter. I value honest and transparent communication, especially with family and friends, as it strengthens our connections and fosters mutual respect.

On the other hand, transparency involves sharing relevant information openly and ensuring everyone understands the decision-making processes, goals, and expectations. This practice reduces misunderstandings, builds accountability, and empowers individuals to contribute meaningfully, knowing they have access to the same information as their leaders. When leaders are transparent, they encourage a culture of collaboration, where feedback is valued and communication flows freely.

Responsibility and Accountability

Responsibility and accountability shape the foundation of real leadership. Responsibility demonstrates a commitment to owning decisions and seeing them through. This involves celebrating successes, acknowledging mistakes, and learning from those experiences. Accountability strengthens this dynamic by ensuring a leader remains answerable to their team and stakeholders. It fosters a culture where everyone feels empowered to contribute, knowing that the leader sets the tone through their integrity and willingness to be held accountable. This approach inspires mutual respect and drives collective achievement.

I would like to take full accountability and responsibility for the results of all my personal and professional responsibilities. I do acknowledge my mistakes with humility and transparency.

Persistence and Resilience

Persistence and resilience are two qualities that are closely linked but serve distinct roles in leadership. Persistence is about maintaining a steady course toward one's goals, regardless of obstacles or setbacks. It is the ability to keep pushing forward, even when progress seems slow or when others might give up. Leaders who embody persistence inspire those around them to stay the course, demonstrating that success often comes to those who do not quit at the first sign of difficulty.

Resilience, however, is the capacity to recover quickly from difficulties. It is about enduring challenges and bouncing back stronger after each setback. Resilient leaders do not just survive hardships; they learn from them, adapt, and use their experiences to propel themselves and their organizations forward. They inspire confidence by showing that failure is not an endpoint but a stage toward future success. Persistence and resilience form the backbone of a leader's journey through adversity, ensuring they reach their goals and grow.

Leaders are supposed to stay positive even when things go tough, make sound decisions in high-pressure situations, and inspire confidence in other teams.

Use of Integrity

Integrity is the bedrock of exemplary leadership. Without it, no amount of skill or knowledge can sustain long-term success. As leaders, we often face choices that test our moral compass. Integrity defines us in those moments, shaping our decisions and legacy.

To lead with integrity means staying true to your principles, even when it is inconvenient. It is about making decisions that align with your core values, not just those that are easy or popular. For me, integrity has always been about honesty and fairness. I strive to be transparent and accountable in every business deal or personal interaction. People follow leaders, and they can trust those who consistently act in line with their stated values.

Leaders who prioritize integrity also foster environments where trust can flourish. This creates a ripple effect, where teams feel safe to take risks, be honest about challenges, and work collaboratively toward shared goals. Integrity breeds credibility, and in leadership, credibility is everything. People are more likely to support, follow, and invest in leaders they believe are conscientious and trustworthy. Leading with integrity is not just the right thing to do; it is a strategic advantage.

Ethical Decision-Making

Ethical decision-making is making choices based on a clear set of moral principles and values, ensuring that actions align with what is right and fair. For a leader, this means considering the broader impact of decisions on the organization, employees, stakeholders, and society. Ethical leaders prioritize integrity over convenience, often opting for the path that may be harder but is morally sound.

I value putting myself in other people's shoes to see the impact on individuals and the community. I like creating and inspiring other people's skills and contributions. I also prioritize transparency, responsibility, and empathy in my decision-making.

A leader who engages in ethical decision-making builds trust and credibility with their immediate team, clients, partners, and the wider community. This approach fosters a culture of fairness and respect, where individuals feel valued and confident in the leadership. Leaders who consistently make ethical choices also set a powerful example for others, demonstrating that success can be achieved without compromising principles. In the long run, ethical decision-making strengthens relationships, ensures long-term stability, and enhances the reputation of both the leader and the organization.

Building Trust

Building trust creates a foundation for meaningful relationships and a collaborative environment. Trust is earned over time through consistent, honest, and transparent actions. When a leader demonstrates reliability by following through on promises, maintaining integrity in difficult situations, and being fair, people are likelier to place their confidence in them.

Leadership depends on building trust, transparency, consistency, and Authenticity. I also like to communicate openly with my employees or mentees. I modeled myself on sharing my vision, challenging the status quo, and encouraging others to act.

A leader builds trust by fostering open communication and showing empathy toward others. Listening actively, addressing concerns, and involving the team in decision-making enhances mutual respect and shows that their opinions matter. Additionally, being accountable for mistakes and willing to learn from them further strengthens trust, reflecting a commitment to growth and fairness.

Trust is not just about leading with authority but about creating a space where people feel safe, respected, and supported. When employees or team members trust their leader, they are more engaged, motivated, and willing to take risks, knowing they have a leader who will back them up. Over time, this trust cultivates loyalty and high performance, benefiting both the individual and the organization.

Commitment to Quality:

Commitment to quality is a defining trait of a dedicated leader. It reflects a leader's dedication to ensuring that every task, project, or goal is executed to the highest standard, no matter the circumstances. A leader committed to quality does not settle for mediocrity. They set high expectations for themselves and their team and continuously strive for improvement.

I want to operate with inclusive leadership. Being a detail-oriented person, 1 do like to appreciate contributions from others, especially if working toward excellence. I continually work toward seeking growth and improvements in any role I am embarking on.

This means paying attention to detail, investing in the right resources, and fostering a culture that values excellence. Leaders who are committed to quality create environments where people are encouraged to take pride in their work. They inspire their teams to go the extra mile by providing feedback, offering additional training, or reinforcing the importance of delivering superior results.

Respect and Fairness

Respect and fairness are cornerstones of effective leadership, creating a foundation of trust and mutual understanding within any team or organization. Leaders who embody respect recognize the inherent value in every individual and treat people with dignity, regardless of their position, background, or differences. Listening actively and considering diverse perspectives foster an environment where people feel valued and heard.

I like fostering team productivity with accelerated growth. This involves providing clear expectations and growth initiatives to my teams or mentees. Likewise, I will promote a shared vision and enable others to act freely. I have used my past adversity and difficult experiences to teach or use other proven models to create a level playing field.

Conversely, fairness ensures that decisions and actions are impartial and based on merit rather than favoritism or bias. Leaders who practice fairness apply the same rules and standards to everyone, ensuring equitable opportunities and transparent processes. They are committed to making just decisions, even when difficult or unpopular. This approach builds trust and promotes a culture of accountability and inclusion.

When leaders demonstrate respect and fairness, they create a positive and productive environment where team members feel empowered to contribute their best work. This sense of equality encourages collaboration, reduces conflicts, and helps build stronger, more cohesive teams.

Leading With Principles

Leadership is not a popularity contest; it is a responsibility to uphold principles that guide actions and decisions. Leading with principles means making choices based on a clear ethical framework rather than being swayed by external pressures or immediate gains. In my journey, I have learned that principles like fairness, respect, and resilience must be at the heart of every decision I make.

A principle-centered leader knows when to take a stand, even when it is unpopular. They balance compassion with firmness, understanding that leadership is more than managing tasks. It is about building a culture of trust and accountability. I have seen the importance of modeling these principles in my personal and professional life. It is not enough to tell others what to do; you must demonstrate it in your actions.

In a business setting, for example, leading with principles has helped me navigate complex situations, from making tough financial decisions to resolving employee conflicts. I have found that when people know that a clear set of values guides their leader, they are more likely to buy into the vision and work toward collective success. This is the power of leading with principles. It elevates the leader and empowers those being led to strive for excellence.

Modeling Desired Behaviors

When leaders exemplify the values, attitudes, and work ethic they wish to see in others, they set a powerful standard for their team to follow. This approach goes beyond simply instructing or dictating; it involves embodying the principles central to the organization's vision and culture.

I like prioritizing team members and setting standards for them and their teams. I want to lead with courage and conviction, intermittently reflecting on my actions and practicing self-awareness with fulfillment of truthfulness and integrity.

Leaders who model the behaviors they expect from their team members build credibility and trust. When employees see that their leader is willing to put in the effort, maintain integrity, and demonstrate a strong work ethic, they are more likely to mirror these actions. It reinforces the idea that expectations are not just for the team but also the leader, creating a sense of shared responsibility and mutual accountability.

Additionally, modeling desired behaviors helps cultivate a positive culture where core values such as respect, professionalism, and collaboration are reinforced daily. Consistency in actions, whether it is showing punctuality, maintaining a positive attitude under pressure, or handling conflicts with grace, leaders can foster an environment where these behaviors become ingrained in the team's practices.

Emotional Intelligence

Emotional intelligence allows leaders to connect with their teams more deeply and manage interpersonal relationships with empathy and understanding. Leaders with high emotional intelligence can recognize their emotions and those of others, using this awareness to guide behavior, resolve conflicts, and inspire their team.

One of the core aspects of emotional intelligence is self-awareness. A leader attuned to their emotional state can regulate their reactions in stressful situations, avoiding impulsive decisions and maintaining composure. This self-control sets a strong example for others, showing that it is possible to manage pressure without compromising professionalism or effectiveness.

Equally important is empathy, which is the ability to understand and share the feelings of others. Leaders who demonstrate empathy build trust and create an inclusive environment where team members feel valued and understood. Moreover, emotional intelligence enhances conflict resolution. Leaders who can read their team's emotional climate are better equipped to navigate disputes, mediate disagreements, and ensure that all parties feel heard and respected. This ability to manage emotions in the workplace improves team dynamics and increases overall job satisfaction and productivity.

Making informed decisions, inspiring innovation, and increasing team productivity were paths of Emotional Intelligence I employed, especially with demonstrating empathy under pressure and considering other emotions.

Strategic Thinking

Strategic thinking aims to steer the team or organization toward long-term success. It involves anticipating future trends, recognizing opportunities and threats, and developing a clear plan to achieve goals. Leaders who engage in strategic thinking are not just focused on immediate tasks or short-term victories; they continuously assess how today's actions align with tomorrow's outcomes.

Strategic thinking requires a leader to maintain a broad perspective. This means understanding the market, industry trends, and the competitive landscape and recognizing internal strengths and weaknesses within the organization. A strategic leader considers all these factors, anticipating potential challenges and opportunities to craft a forward-looking plan.

I would occasionally look beyond today's issue and think long term, especially when we got into the real estate business and later with providing mortgage services to the low- and middle-class-income groups, knowing fully well that there might be greater rewards in the long-term but providing capital now to a fixed project. I like to think of generational wealth rather than just creating wealth. I like to foster a culture of innovation and continuous improvement.

Another key element is flexibility. While strategic thinkers set clear goals and map out a pathway to achieve them, they also recognize that change is inevitable. The best strategies are adaptable. A leader must remain open to revisiting and revising plans based on new information, unexpected developments, or evolving circumstances. Strategic thinking, therefore, combines vision with agility, allowing leaders to pivot when necessary without losing sight of long-term objectives.

Strategic thinking also emphasizes data-driven decision-making. Leaders who practice this skill make informed choices, relying on research, data analysis, and careful risk assessment. They avoid basing decisions solely on gut instinct or reactionary measures. This approach ensures that every action taken is calculated, purposeful, and aligned with the organization's mission.

Efficiency and Effectiveness

Efficiency and effectiveness are two key pillars of successful leadership, each playing a distinct role in managing resources and achieving goals. Efficiency refers to the ability to accomplish tasks with minimal waste of time, effort, or resources, while effectiveness focuses on achieving the right goals and outcomes. A successful leader must balance both to ensure their team or organization works swiftly and meets its objectives.

I prefer taking risks and experimenting with new ideas. I also create a vision for the future and inspire others to work toward achieving it. I encourage leadership by building trust among my teams or mentees.

Leaders who emphasize efficiency are adept at recognizing bottlenecks and finding ways to improve productivity without overburdening their team. This could mean adopting new technologies, refining systems, or delegating tasks to those best suited to handling them. Efficiency is crucial because it allows an organization to operate smoothly and with agility, freeing up resources that can be reinvested elsewhere.

Effectiveness, on the other hand, is about doing the right things. It is not just about how quickly or well tasks are completed but whether they align with the organization's goals. Leaders who prioritize effectiveness are clear about the organization's mission and ensure that every effort is directed toward advancing it. They focus on high-impact activities, ensuring the team's energy is spent on what matters most.

When efficiency and effectiveness are combined, the results are powerful. A leader who cultivates both ensures that their team is not only working hard but also working smart. Projects are completed on time and within budget, but more importantly, they drive the organization forward meaningfully. This balance prevents wasted effort on low-priority tasks while ensuring that key goals are met in the most resourceful manner possible.

Building and Leading Teams

The success of their team measures a leader's true impact. Building and leading a team is one of leadership's most challenging yet rewarding aspects. It requires technical skills, emotional intelligence, fostering collaboration, and a deep understanding of what motivates individuals to work toward a shared goal.

To build an effective team, a leader must first create an environment of trust. This means encouraging open communication, valuing diverse perspectives, and ensuring that each team member feels their contributions are recognized and valued. Trust is the foundation upon which strong teams are built; collaboration quickly breaks down without it. I have always made it a point to be accessible to my team, to listen actively, and to create opportunities for everyone to contribute their ideas.

Leading a team also involves understanding the dynamics of conflict and resolution. No team is immune to disagreements, but exemplary leaders can navigate these challenges with diplomacy and fairness. Conflict, when managed well, can lead to growth and innovation. My approach has always been to address issues head-on, encouraging constructive dialogue and ensuring that all voices are heard.

Team Dynamics and Collaboration

Team dynamics and collaboration are crucial elements in the success of any group or organization. A team's strength lies in its collective synergy, the ability of individuals to work together harmoniously, bringing out the best in one another while working towards a common goal. Team dynamics refers to how individuals in a group interact, communicate, and cooperate, while collaboration focuses on leveraging the strengths of each member to achieve shared objectives.

This involves intricately interweaving every facet of existence with innovation to productivity without compromising employees' overall success and satisfaction. It includes diversity and inclusion, conflict resolution, factoring in team personalities, and different roles and responsibilities.

Strong team dynamics are built on mutual respect, trust, and a clear understanding of each team member's roles and responsibilities. Leaders who foster positive team dynamics create an environment where individuals feel valued and understood. This, in turn, encourages open communication, creativity, and a willingness to share ideas without fear of judgment. Leaders play a pivotal role in managing conflicts that may arise, ensuring they are resolved constructively and preventing any disruption to the team's workflow or morale.

Conversely, collaboration brings together a group's diverse skills and talents to generate better outcomes than individuals working in isolation. A leader's role in collaboration involves encouraging cross-functional teamwork, where individuals from different departments or areas of expertise come together to offer their insights. In doing so, leaders create a space where knowledge-sharing becomes a powerful tool, leading to innovative solutions and improved decision-making.

Fostering strong team dynamics and encouraging collaboration has immense benefits. Teams that function well together can respond quickly to challenges, adapt to changes, and push the organization forward through cohesive efforts. The leader's ability to recognize the value of diversity within the team, whether in terms of skills, perspectives, or experiences, enhances the group's problem-solving capacity and overall performance.

Conflict Resolution

Conflict resolution is vital for any leader, as conflicts are inevitable in team settings, workplaces, or any group of individuals working together. It involves constructively addressing disagreements, misunderstandings, or tensions, allowing all parties to feel heard and respected. It is not just about settling disputes but finding solutions that promote harmony and strengthen relationships rather than causing lingering resentment or division.

A leader's role in conflict resolution begins with creating an open environment where individuals feel comfortable expressing their concerns without fear of retribution. Encouraging open communication allows potential conflicts to surface early, making it easier to address them before they escalate. When conflicts arise, a leader must remain neutral and listen actively to all sides. Understanding the root cause of the conflict is essential, as it often goes beyond surface disagreements to deeper issues like miscommunication, unmet needs, or clashing values.

Once the problem is identified, a leader must guide the involved parties toward a solution by encouraging compromise, mutual understanding, and collaboration. The goal is to find a fair and acceptable resolution for all, which may require finding common ground or exploring alternative approaches. Empathy plays a key role in this process, as it helps the leader and team members appreciate different perspectives and motivations.

When resolving a conflict, I pay attention to what everyone is saying, try to understand the causes and focus more on problem-solving than people. I like to consider others' Perspectives and points of view. I try my best to be nonjudgmental in my approach to conflict resolution but empathize with others' feelings. I also prefer acting fast on solutions and putting systems in place to monitor progress.

Leaders must also be firm when necessary, ensuring the resolution is consistent with the team's goals, values, and standards. This may mean enforcing certain rules or boundaries, particularly if the conflict involves behavior that undermines the team's cohesion or performance. However, the resolution process should remain as transparent as possible so all team members understand the rationale behind the decisions.

The advantages of helpful conflict resolution are manifold. It leads to stronger relationships, greater trust, and enhanced team dynamics as individuals learn to work through their differences healthily. It also fosters a more positive work environment where creativity and collaboration flourish, as people feel safe and supported in expressing their ideas or concerns. Moreover, successful conflict resolution equips a team with resilience, allowing them to navigate future challenges more effectively.

Celebrating Success

When leaders acknowledge and celebrate achievements, big or small, they convey that hard work, dedication, and contributions are valued. This recognition motivates individuals to continue performing at a high level and strengthens the sense of camaraderie and shared purpose within the group.

Celebrating success begins with recognizing milestones, whether individual achievements like meeting personal development goals or exceeding performance expectations or collective accomplishments such as completing a project or hitting key targets.

To help the team reflect on their progress and encourage them further, I focus on boosting morale by celebrating achievements and fostering camaraderie. I do this by giving awards, organizing team outings, hosting catered luncheons, and sharing success stories to inspire others.

Additionally, I offer bonuses to reward hard work and promote success within the system.

In the fast-paced work environment, it is easy to focus solely on what still needs to be done and overlook the progress already made. Taking time to celebrate helps leaders shift focus to the positive, renewing energy and enthusiasm. It also helps the team maintain perspective, recognizing that while challenges exist, they can overcome them together.

When success is rewarded, it encourages others to strive for similar recognition. It sets a benchmark for excellence and inspires healthy competition and personal growth within the team. Leaders can use celebrations as a teaching moment, pointing out the behaviors, skills, and decisions that led to success and encouraging others to adopt similar approaches.

Sustaining Leadership Through Change

Sustaining leadership through change requires adaptability, resilience, and clear communication. Effective leaders anticipate change and prepare their teams for it by fostering a culture of flexibility and open-mindedness. They communicate the reasons behind the changes and guide their team through uncertainty with clarity and empathy. Additionally, they provide the tools and resources needed to help the team transition smoothly, ensuring everyone feels supported throughout the process.

Leaders are crucial in keeping their teams focused, motivated, and aligned with the organization's evolving goals. By embracing adaptability, they strengthen their team's trust in leadership and help them recognize and seize new opportunities that come with change.

I envision creating a future grounded in human dignity and an atmosphere of trust. I find fulfillment in empowering others, remaining open to new ideas, maintaining a positive outlook, and demonstrating resilience in overcoming challenges. Encouraging others and fostering a strong team spirit are values I hold dearly as a leader.

Global Leadership Insights

Leadership Through Sacrifice

Great leaders often demonstrate selflessness, putting the needs of others ahead of their own. The willingness to sacrifice personal gain for the greater good is a hallmark of responsible leadership. Leaders willing to serve others, especially in difficult circumstances, gain trust and inspire their team to do the same. Sacrifice in leadership builds credibility, which is essential for long-term influence.

Building Resilience Through Adversity

Leaders who succeed through challenges understand that adversity strengthens their leadership. Resilience is not just about enduring hardship but learning from it and using those lessons to build a stronger foundation in the face of obstacles. Leaders create an environment where others feel empowered to overcome challenges and remain focused on collective goals.

Transparency as a Foundation for Trust

Openness and honesty in communication are key to building trust within teams and organizations. Leaders who practice transparency make decisions based on integrity, leading to a culture of respect. When team members are confident in their leader's honesty, they are more likely to contribute fully, knowing they are valued and part of something meaningful. Transparency fosters loyalty and commitment.

Accountability as a Leadership Pillar

A strong leader holds themselves accountable for their decisions and actions. By accepting responsibility for positive and negative outcomes, leaders set a standard for the entire organization. Accountability ensures that leaders are not above the rules but are committed to fairness and ethical conduct, creating a culture where people are motivated to meet high-performance standards.

Sustaining Growth Through Adaptability

Change is inevitable in personal and professional realms, and leaders who adapt to evolving circumstances are better positioned to drive long-term success. Leading through change requires flexibility, optimism, and a willingness to embrace new ideas while staying true to core values. Adaptability ensures that leadership remains dynamic, responsive, and forward-looking, inspiring others to embrace transformation confidently.

Conclusion

Exemplary leadership is more than the sum of the principles it embodies; it is a continuous commitment to inspiring, uplifting, and creating lasting change. The power of integrity, team building, and leading with purpose is the bedrock for navigating future aspirations.

As we focus on the future, we will explore how these guiding values shape personal ambitions, family legacies, and broader community engagements, all while setting the stage for a global impact that reaches far beyond our immediate surroundings.

CHAPTER 11

FUTURE GOALS AND ASPIRATIONS

FUTURE GOALS AND ASPIRATIONS guide one's personal and professional life toward meaningful growth and fulfillment. They mirror a person's vision for what they hope to achieve, how they want to impact the world, and the legacy they intend to leave behind. For a leader, these goals often go beyond personal success, extending into community service, global influence, and mentorship.

Aspirations provide the drive to pursue new heights in career advancements, personal development, or contributing to the greater good. They require a balance of ambition, strategic planning, and perseverance, helping individuals shape a future that aligns with their values, dreams, and the positive changes they hope to create.

Personal Ambitions

My ambition has always been centered around being a blessing to others. True fulfillment comes from extending a helping hand to the world to offer something meaningful to those in need. Throughout my professional journey, this belief has guided me toward a path where I can serve humanity, especially through my chosen field of physical therapy.

I have been fortunate to reach the pinnacle of my profession, having earned my doctoral degree in physical therapy. This accomplishment allows me to support individuals with various musculoskeletal conditions and disabilities, helping them elevate their pain and reclaim their lives.

It is a privilege to assist those who struggle, and my joy lies not in the financial reward but in seeing the positive impact on my patients' lives. Helping others achieve their goals and relieve their pain is the fulfillment of my professional ambition and the reason I pursued this career in the first place.

Personal Development

Alongside my professional success, personal development has been a vital aspect of my journey. Every step of the way, I have fortified myself with knowledge gained from studying, attending seminars, and engaging with like-minded individuals. Networking with colleagues, friends, and family has expanded my horizons.

I am a lifelong learner, always eager to read, explore, and understand more about the world and the challenges people face. Reading biographies of remarkable individuals has been a significant source of inspiration, offering me insight into how others have navigated their paths and overcome obstacles. Their stories fuel my drive to continue learning, growing, and contributing to the world around me.

I am constantly seeking ways to improve myself, to be more creative, and to learn from others. While I admire the accomplishments of those who have gone before me, I am not one to follow a well-worn path. I prefer to create new paths, innovate, and challenge myself uniquely. Like Elon Musk, I embrace creativity, knowing failure is part of the process. Even if I fall seven times, I believe in standing up eight. This approach has allowed me to cultivate resilience and embrace opportunities with an open mind.

Health and Wellness

Health and wellness have become central to my development as I grow older. I have learned the importance of paying close attention to my body, listening to its needs, and adjusting to ensure I remain physically, mentally, and emotionally in peak condition. I focus on maintaining a balanced lifestyle, including proper nutrition, regular exercise, and sufficient sleep. The long hours of my professional life and the responsibilities of family and personal ambitions can be demanding. Still, I have realized that prioritizing health is key to sustaining everything else.

Regarding physical wellness, I believe in simple routines that go a long way: eating healthy meals, engaging in regular physical activity, and resting. A disciplined approach to wellness has helped me stay energetic and focused. I often joke with colleagues about how we all rush home to collapse on the couch after a long day, but even in those moments of rest, I am mindful of giving my body what it needs to recover and recharge.

Mental and emotional wellness are equally important to me. In the fast-paced, often stressful environment, I work in, it is crucial to take moments of pause, whether through prayer, meditation, or simply walking in the quiet of the early morning. These practices help me manage stress and keep a clear mind, ready to handle the day's challenges. By carving out time for these moments of solitude and reflection, I keep anxiety at bay and maintain a positive, resilient outlook on life.

Health and wellness are not just about the absence of illness but about creating a lifestyle that supports longevity, joy, and balance. Whether through physical care, mindfulness practices, or simply enjoying a peaceful walk, I strive to nurture every aspect of my well-being to continue to pursue my goals and ambitions with full vitality.

Creative Pursuits

Creativity has always fueled my desire to explore the world. Ever since my high school days, geography has fascinated me. It opened doors to places I had never been, sparking my ambition to see the world's wonders. Even now, I dream of visiting countries like Canada, Australia, and Israel, marveling at the Pyramids of Egypt, and standing in awe of nature's most magnificent landscapes.

My travels have taken me across three continents: Africa, North America, and Europe, but there is still much to explore. Asia, Japan, China, and other corners of the world remain on my list of destinations to experience. For me, travel is more than just a pastime. It is an opportunity to appreciate the vastness of creation, witness the beauty of our world, and broaden my horizons in ways that enrich my personal and professional life. Exploring new places and cultures is a passion that inspires my creativity and personal growth.

Family and Relationships

Family has always been the cornerstone of my life, shaping my values, providing emotional support, and grounding me in times of uncertainty. My wife and children are the pillars of my strength, offering a sanctuary I can always return to, no matter the challenges I face in the outside world. The bond we share, built on mutual respect and love, has been instrumental in helping me maintain a balanced life while pursuing my professional and personal ambitions.

One of my long-standing goals has been to foster strong family ties within my nuclear family and with extended family members. I come from a family deeply rooted in tradition, and these values must be passed on to my children. As much as I have embraced modern living and life in different parts of the world, I always emphasize the importance of staying connected to our heritage. I encourage my children to cherish relationships beyond our immediate household.

Building a legacy is another key aspect of my family life. I want to leave behind more than material wealth; I want to leave behind a legacy of values of honesty, integrity, resilience, and compassion that my children and future generations can carry forward. This is why I intentionally create lasting memories and instill values that can be passed on. Whether through simple family traditions, shared meals, or life lessons that arise in day-to-day conversations,

I aim to impart wisdom that will guide my children long after I am gone.

I have also learned that widening networks, both socially and professionally, contributes to the strength of family. My relationships with friends, mentors, and colleagues are extensions of my family, offering different perspectives and support systems that enrich my life. I nurture these relationships with care, maintain communication, offer support, and seek advice when needed. I find the balance between personal fulfillment and professional growth in these networks, knowing that both are intertwined and vital for a well-rounded life.

Communication is at the heart of everything, whether with my wife, children, extended family, or friends. Open and honest communication forms the foundation of strong relationships, allowing us to understand each other better and navigate life's challenges with unity and trust. I hold this dearly, as it ensures that even as life becomes more complex, the core of who we are and what we value remains intact. In the end, the strength of these relationships sustains us and gives us the resilience to keep moving forward.

Community Engagement

Looking ahead, one of my most important goals is to give back to the community meaningfully. I have always believed that success is not measured solely by personal achievements, but by the impact one has on others. In this next phase of my life, I am committed to deepening my involvement in community-based activities, philanthropy, and mentorship, contributing to the well-being of society in various ways.

Philanthropy and Volunteering

I believe that to whom much is given, much is expected. My desire to give back stems from a deep gratitude for the opportunities I have been afforded. As I move forward, my goal is to increase my philanthropic efforts, whether through financial contributions, volunteering my time, or creating programs that support underserved populations.

It is not just about writing checks; it is about rolling up my sleeves and being directly involved in causes that align with my values, whether supporting education, healthcare, or other social initiatives. I envision continuing to work with my foundation, creating new projects that provide educational scholarships and healthcare services to those in need.

I prioritize staying active, both within my church and through philanthropic efforts. I am deeply involved in leadership in the church and serve as a Sunday school teacher, guiding others in their spiritual growth. Our congregation is large, with over six hundred members, and I am also part of the Men of Elon Executive team. We have various initiatives, including a business channel that connects our members and other community-focused programs.

Our church plays an impactful role in the city where we live, and we pride ourselves on being a strong part of the community. We organize family connections and fellowships, which bring people together and foster relationships. I lead a small group in our church where we study different books, discuss their lessons, and apply them to our personal and spiritual lives. We are reviewing *The 21 Irrefutable Laws of Leadership* by John Maxwell for October. This is one of the many books we have studied in our small group, and it is an example of my passion for continuous learning. I enjoy reading and exploring new ideas, which I believe always opens doors to new beginnings and opportunities for growth.

Mentorship and Coaching

One of the most rewarding aspects of my life has been the opportunity to mentor and coach others. I plan to expand my role as a mentor, particularly for young professionals and aspiring entrepreneurs. I want to share my journey, the lessons I have learned, and the strategies I have developed for overcoming obstacles.

Mentorship is not only about giving advice; it is about guiding others as they chart their path, offering support when needed, and celebrating their successes. I see this as a crucial part of my legacy, helping to cultivate the next generation of leaders by investing in their growth and success.

I often mentor junior colleagues and assistants who shadow me on the job. It is a mutually beneficial experience; they learn from me, and I learn from them. Over the years, I have had many assistants and mentees, and we have built a strong network.

It is remarkable how these connections have lasted. Whether in Michigan, another state where I have practiced, or even visiting London, I still maintain friendships with many of the professionals I have worked with. We stay in touch, share experiences, and support each other. These enduring relationships are a testament to the value of networking, collaboration, and the bonds formed through mentorship.

Public Speaking and Advocacy

Another way I hope to engage with my community is through public speaking and advocacy. In the coming years, I aspire to speak more openly about my life's challenges and triumphs, sharing insights on leadership, entrepreneurship, and resilience.

Whether at local events, conferences, or online platforms, I see myself becoming more vocal on issues close to my heart, especially education, healthcare, and immigrant success. Advocacy will allow me to amplify the voices of those who are often unheard of and ensure that more people have access to the resources and opportunities they need to succeed.

We regularly review our goals, and I often participate in public speaking and advocacy efforts. Despite my strong Nigerian accent, I am particularly passionate about this area. I have never shied away from it, but I know it might make me self-conscious in certain settings. However, my desire to give back and impact, especially in Nigeria, drives me. I would love to return home and inspire my people, speak to them about my experiences, and encourage them to pursue their ambitions.

In addition to public speaking, I have also found myself increasingly drawn to academia. Teaching, consulting, and sharing my knowledge with future leaders is something I would love to explore, especially as I approach retirement. I will be turning sixty next year, and as I transition into the next phase of life, I want to remain active in advocacy and mentorship, helping the next generation find their path and succeed in their careers.

Collaborations with Community Leaders

My book focuses on leadership. I have always believed that while some leaders are born, leadership is also a skill that can be developed and refined over time. Even now, I am still learning and evolving in different areas of leadership. There are so many facets to it that I am continuously exploring, and it is one area where I want to leave a lasting impact on the world.

I want to learn from others and teach those who come after me, ensuring we leave a legacy of strong, compassionate, and effective leadership. I am particularly passionate about collaboration with community leaders. Working together to create a positive impact, foster growth, and develop leadership skills in others is where I feel I can make a real difference. It is not just about leading in the professional sphere but about making meaningful contributions to the communities I am a part of.

Global Impact

Global impact has always been central to my vision, so my company is OKUNS Global. The name reflects our ambition's scope: we are not confined by geographical boundaries. In today's world, technology has made it possible for anyone, anywhere, to reach you, learn about your work, and connect with you. This is the foundation of my approach to widening networks, personally and professionally.

I envision being recognized globally, much like renowned figures such as Warren Buffet, who are known for their stock-picking expertise. I want people to know me for what I stand for, whether it is in healthcare, entrepreneurship, or leadership. I aim to extend my reach into every corner of the world, empowering others.

Communication is key, especially when empowering the next generation of leaders. Strong communication builds connections, spreads knowledge, and strengthens networks. Through my ventures, like our medical equipment company, the focus is not solely on profit. Yes, we run a business, but we also aim to use it as a vehicle to give back, especially to those in need, such as older people and people with disabilities. We donate essential products like walkers and wheelchairs to people in Africa and other third-world countries through partnerships and global networking.

This is where my foundation also comes into play. Our goal is to blend profit with purpose. By collaborating with other large companies and creating a network of resources, we aim to provide for those who lack access to basic healthcare equipment. In the process, we are not just offering physical tools but also building stronger communities and empowering people in places where resources are scarce. I believe the ripple effect of this work will leave a lasting global impact.

Global Leadership Insights

Purpose-Driven Ambition

A true global leader is motivated by a purpose beyond personal success. Leaders can inspire and uplift those around them by aligning their ambitions with the greater good through professional excellence, personal development, or creative exploration. Purpose-driven goals create a ripple effect that encourages others to pursue their ambitions with integrity and determination.

Embrace Continuous Learning

Lifelong learning is key to staying relevant in a constantly changing world. Leaders must remain adaptable by investing in personal and professional growth, seeking knowledge from diverse sources, and being open to new ideas. Personal development is not a one-time achievement but a continuous process that empowers leaders to face challenges head-on and lead effectively across different environments.

Legacy Through Family and Relationships

Building a strong family foundation and nurturing relationships is essential for a leader's long-term vision. Creating a legacy pertains not only to career achievements but also to the values passed on to future generations. Family bonds, trust, and communication are critical in shaping a leader's personal and professional life approach, ensuring their influence surpasses their immediate circle.

Philanthropy and Community Engagement as a Leadership Responsibility

Global leaders understand that their impact reaches beyond business success. Leaders set an example of social responsibility by engaging with communities, participating in philanthropy, and encouraging mentorship. Community engagement fosters a deeper connection with others, allowing leaders to give back, share knowledge, and create lasting change in the lives of others.

Global Vision and Network Building

A global mindset is essential in today's interconnected world. Leaders who actively seek opportunities to expand their networks, collaborate across borders, and engage in cultural exchanges can leverage their influence on a global scale. Networking across different cultures and industries allows leaders to drive innovation, share knowledge, and create opportunities far beyond local environments.

Conclusion

Personal ambition intertwined with community engagement leads to natural progression, which creates platforms that turn these aspirations into impactful realities. The Okunrounmu Foundation and OKUNS GLOBAL Enterprises exemplify this vision, where the drive to empower others and build global connections is channeled into meaningful actions.

Rooted in a commitment to social responsibility and innovation, these initiatives showcase how personal passion can evolve into ventures that inspire change and foster sustainable growth across communities. Let us investigate how these endeavors pave the way for a broader global impact.

VENTURE INTO A GLOBAL ENTITY

CHAPTER 12

THE OKUNROUNMU FOUNDATION AND OKUNSGLOBAL ENTERPRISES

The Vision and Mission of Okunrounmu Foundation

The vision continues to expand from the beginnings of personal ambition to creating meaningful community and global impacts. The Okunrounmu Foundation and OKUNS GLOBAL Enterprises exemplify how entrepreneurial leadership can give back to society while fostering business growth. These initiatives reflect a desire for success and a commitment to create lasting change in people's lives, particularly through education, healthcare, and sustainable business practices. Let us venture into more detail.

Founding Principles:

The Okunrounmu Foundation was born out of the desire to make a tangible difference in the lives of underserved communities, particularly in Nigeria and other parts of Africa. The foundation is built on compassion, empowerment, and a deep commitment to uplifting the less fortunate. Inspired by personal experiences of overcoming adversity, the foundation seeks to extend a helping hand to individuals who lack access to essential resources such as education and healthcare.

The founding principle is simple: to use every opportunity to give back to society. Whether through mentorship, financial support, or creating educational programs, the Okunrounmu Foundation is committed to improving the quality of life for those in need.

Core Objectives

The foundation's objectives are built around a few key areas:

Education: Offering scholarships and educational programs to children and young adults who demonstrate potential but lack the financial means to pursue their education.

Healthcare: Providing medical assistance, equipment, and outreach programs, especially in rural areas where access to healthcare is limited.

Community Empowerment: Supporting local businesses, vocational training, and entrepreneurship to foster self-reliance and reduce poverty.

Environmental Sustainability: Promoting initiatives that protect the environment and encourage the sustainable use of natural resources.

Impact and Achievements

Since its inception, the Okunrounmu Foundation has touched the lives of many individuals, particularly in rural Nigeria. The foundation has partnered with local schools to provide scholarships, distribute medical equipment to underserved hospitals, and run health outreach programs that educate communities on preventive care. These initiatives have provided immediate relief and laid the groundwork for long-term growth and development within these communities.

Expanding Reach and Scope

The foundation's vision continues to grow, with plans to expand its reach beyond Nigeria to other parts of Africa and other continents. As the foundation matures, it aims to broaden its impact through more structured partnerships with international organizations, governments, and private sector entities. The goal is to create a sustainable, scalable model that empowers communities to take charge of their futures.

Key Initiatives and Projects

Any business must go beyond providing products or services to thrive and make a lasting impact. Initiatives and projects offer businesses an avenue to give back to their communities and foster growth, innovation, and long-term sustainability. These initiatives allow companies to address broader social and environmental challenges, cultivate positive brand recognition, and engage with the public more personally.

At OKUNS GLOBAL, these initiatives form a core part of the company's mission. Understanding that business success is not solely measured by profit, OKUNS GLOBAL integrates key projects that impact education, healthcare, community development, and environmental sustainability into its operations. These initiatives reflect the company's commitment to creating value for society while reinforcing its role as a responsible corporate entity.

Among OKUNS GLOBAL's signature projects are:

Educational Programs: OKUNS GLOBAL believes in the power of education to transform lives. The company runs programs to foster learning opportunities for underprivileged youth in Nigeria and beyond. By providing scholarships and educational resources, OKUNS GLOBAL is helping to shape future generations and empower them with the tools for success.

Healthcare Initiatives: Acknowledging the critical importance of access to quality healthcare, OKUNS GLOBAL is committed to providing medical equipment and services in the U.S. and African communities. The company's initiative to donate essential medical supplies such as wheelchairs and walkers to underserved populations is a testament to its dedication to improving lives and making healthcare accessible.

Community Development: OKUNS GLOBAL engages in community-building projects to uplift neighborhoods and create SUSTAINABLE development. These initiatives include improving local infrastructure, supporting small businesses, and providing financial assistance for community-driven projects. The company's focus on community growth demonstrates its belief in creating shared value for the areas it serves.

Environmental Sustainability: Recognizing the importance of protecting the planet for future generations, OKUNS GLOBAL is actively involved in projects that promote environmental sustainability. Through its business operations and community outreach, the company encourages practices that reduce waste, conserve resources, and promote eco-friendly solutions. OKUNS GLOBAL's environmental initiatives are designed to align business growth with the environment's well-being.

In running these initiatives, OKUNS GLOBAL fulfills its corporate social responsibility and strengthens its connection with its customers and communities. These projects reflect the company's values, offering tangible benefits to society while enhancing OKUNS GLOBAL's reputation as a leader in business and philanthropy.

The OKUNS GLOBAL Enterprise

OKUNS GLOBAL Enterprises was created to expand the influence of the Okunrounmu family's business acumen beyond national borders. Initially founded as a small enterprise, the company has grown into a multifaceted entity with real estate, healthcare services, and retail operations. However, the path to success was not without its challenges.

The business began in 2009 when *OKUNS Investment LLC* was first established in Michigan, followed by the creation of *OKUNS Global Nigerian Limited* in 2005. As operations grew, the company relocated to Georgia in 2017, merging all ventures under the single brand, *OKUNS GLOBAL Incorporated*, in 2019. Yet, throughout these expansions, the company faced significant obstacles, including financial constraints, regulatory hurdles, and intense competition in the U.S. and Nigeria.

One of the greatest challenges was establishing credibility in international markets while navigating new business environments. Building trust and a reputable brand requires financial investment, personal sacrifice, and continuous learning. Despite these challenges, the company's strong foundation and adaptability allowed it to persevere.

Business Ideology

A company's business ideology forms the foundation upon which its operations, strategies, and interactions are built. The guiding philosophy influences decision-making, shapes corporate culture, and determines commitment to customers, employees, and communities. Successful businesses are driven by clear and purposeful ideologies emphasizing integrity, innovation, and sustainability.

A strong business ideology defines a company's internal ethos and informs its external relationships, helping to build trust, loyalty, and long-term success in an ever-changing market. This shared set of values serves as the compass that guides companies through challenges while enabling them to maintain a positive impact on society.

A commitment to quality, innovation, and integrity is at the heart of OKUNS GLOBAL's business ideology. The company prides itself on offering exceptional products and services in every market. Whether in healthcare, real estate, or retail, OKUNS GLOBAL aims to set new standards for excellence.

OKUNS GLOBAL Enterprises has a vision of creating value for its customers, employees, and society. The corporate culture unites its workforce with a shared purpose: to be competitive without compromising quality. OKUNS GLOBAL believes in celebrating achievers, embracing diverse cultures, and prioritizing customer satisfaction. The company's mission is to serve as a trusted global partner, delivering excellence across multiple sectors.

Social responsibility remains a cornerstone of OKUNS GLOBAL's business philosophy. Through various charitable endeavors and community service initiatives, the company ensures it gives back to its societies, reinforcing its role as a business and a positive force for social change.

Services and Products

A business's services and products are tangible expressions of its mission and values, reflecting its commitment to addressing customer needs and contributing to the marketplace. These offerings are the key touchpoints between a business and its clients, defining the customer experience and often serving as a competitive advantage. A diverse range of services and products allows a business to reach multiple markets, adapt to changing economic conditions, and cater to evolving consumer demands.

Companies that excel in developing high-quality, innovative offerings often gain trust and loyalty, positioning themselves as leaders within their industry. Services and products are the backbone of a business's revenue stream and a testament to its ability to deliver value and maintain relevance in a competitive landscape.

OKUNS GLOBAL offers a wide range of products and services, including:

Real estate development and property management, with properties in the U.S. and Nigeria, spanning five states in Nigeria.

Healthcare services, including rehabilitation and home care contracts with nursing homes, hospitals, and individual home care clients.

Retail operations, such as *OKUNS Medical Equipment Company*, which sells and rents medical supplies like walkers, wheelchairs, and other essential items. The company has also expanded its offerings to rental services in event planning, beauty care, and adult foster care.

In addition, OKUNS GLOBAL provides financial services through its *OKUNS Mortgage Unit* and personal and business loan services in Nigeria. The company's business model diversifies its income streams, making it a key player across multiple industries and markets.

Market Expansion

Market expansion is a strategic approach that businesses use to grow their influence, increase their customer base, and enhance profitability. Entering new markets, geographically or demographically, enables companies to diversify their revenue streams and mitigate risks associated with over-reliance on a single market. Expanding into different regions or sectors opens new opportunities, encourages innovation, and provides access to a broader customer base.

Successful market expansion requires thorough research, adaptation to local regulations and cultures, and anticipating market trends. Ensuring long-term sustainability and growth is critical, allowing businesses to remain competitive and relevant in an increasingly globalized economy.

OKUNS GLOBAL has experienced substantial growth in recent years, establishing a global footprint while remaining rooted in the Nigerian and American markets. The company is headquartered in Georgia, with a store located at 6525 Tara Boulevard in Jonesboro, and has developed a strong presence through its online platform at www.okunsglobal.com.

The business strategy is built on continuous expansion, leveraging technology to reach global markets. OKUNS

GLOBAL operates with low overhead costs and a commission-based contractor system, ensuring operational efficiency and sustainability. The company actively seeks new opportunities in emerging markets, especially across Africa, and has a growing interest in international business ventures, cultural exchanges, and cross-border collaborations.

Looking ahead, OKUNS GLOBAL's goal is to solidify its position as a global brand. Through its diverse operations, innovative services, and commitment to social responsibility, the company strives to make a lasting impact on the global stage.

Business Expansion and Innovations

These are fundamental drivers of long-term growth and sustainability for any enterprise. Expansion often involves scaling operations, entering new markets, or diversifying product lines, allowing companies to capitalize on emerging opportunities and customer demands. On the other hand, innovation is the creative engine behind staying competitive, whether developing new products, adopting cutting-edge technology, or refining business processes.

By continuously evolving and embracing change, businesses enhance their market position and foster resilience in industry shifts. The synergy between expansion and innovation propels companies toward higher efficiency, greater customer satisfaction, and overall success in an ever-changing global marketplace.

OKUNS GLOBAL's growth has been carefully planned through several strategic decisions. The company continuously assesses market trends and consumer needs to stay ahead of the curve. Expansion into new industries, such as renewable energy and technology, is part of its future roadmap.

As part of its innovation commitment, OKUNS GLOBAL invests in technology-driven solutions. The company understands that staying relevant requires embracing the latest advancements, from healthcare technologies that improve patient care to real estate innovations that enhance sustainable living.

Targeted Partnerships and Collaborations:

Partnerships and collaborations are vital for businesses aiming to broaden their reach, access new markets, and enhance their capabilities. By forming strategic alliances, companies can pool resources, share expertise, and leverage complementary strengths to achieve common goals.

Collaborations often provide access to innovative technologies, new customer bases, and fresh perspectives, fostering growth and creating opportunities that might be difficult to achieve independently. In a globalized world, partnerships enable businesses to adapt quickly to market demands and navigate complex challenges, ensuring sustainable growth and long-term success.

OKUNS GLOBAL's success has been due to its ability to forge meaningful partnerships. By collaborating with international companies, government entities, and NGOs, the company has scaled its operations and expanded its influence. The company always seeks new partnerships that align with its mission and vision.

Corporate Social Responsibility (CSR)

Corporate Social Responsibility (CSR) refers to a company's efforts to operate ethically, sustainably, and with a community focus. Businesses that adopt CSR initiatives recognize their responsibility to generate profit and contribute positively to society. This can include environmental sustainability efforts, philanthropy, ethical labor practices, and community engagement.

Integrating CSR into their operations builds trust with customers, employees, and stakeholders, enhances their brand reputation, and makes a tangible impact on the world. Effective CSR initiatives can strengthen relationships, create goodwill, and foster a sense of purpose beyond financial success.

A deep commitment to corporate social responsibility is at the core of OKUNS GLOBAL's operations. The company believes that businesses have a responsibility to contribute positively to society. Whether through environmental sustainability initiatives, charitable donations, or community outreach programs, OKUNS GLOBAL aims to influence the world while building a successful enterprise.

Global Leadership Insights

Embrace Global Vision and Local Impact:

OKUNS GLOBAL embodies the power of combining a global mindset with a deep commitment to local communities. Its reach across continents is expanding while keeping the well-being of local populations at the forefront; the company serves as a model for businesses that aspire to influence global markets without losing sight of their roots. OKUNS GLOBAL's successful healthcare, real estate, and retail ventures demonstrate that businesses can make a global impact with the right vision while fostering local change.

Innovative Solutions for Complex Challenges

OKUNSGLOBAL's growth is a testament to the power of innovation in addressing market challenges. The company has created solutions that resonate across industries and geographies by integrating new technologies, responding to customer needs, and continuously evolving its business model. As a leader in U.S. and Nigerian markets, OKUNSGLOBAL provides tailored, innovative services that set new standards for excellence, encouraging clients to engage with a business that thrives on creativity and forward-thinking.

A Commitment to Social Responsibility:

At OKUNS GLOBAL, success is measured not solely by profit margins but by the positive impact on communities. Through its philanthropic initiatives, healthcare services for underserved populations, and environmental sustainability efforts, OKUNS GLOBAL is committed to giving back to the society in which it operates. By choosing OKUNS GLOBAL, clients and partners align themselves with a company that believes in the power of ethical business practices and responsible leadership.

Strategic Partnerships for Global Growth:

OKUNSGLOBAL's strength lies in its ability to build meaningful partnerships that transcend borders. The company has expanded its influence and offers unique services across different markets. Clients who seek out OKUNS GLOBAL tap into a network of experts who deliver results through strategic, innovative partnerships, ensuring sustained growth and mutual success.

Leadership Built on Integrity and Innovation:

OKUNS GLOBAL's leadership sets the tone for its global success, emphasizing integrity, resilience, and a commitment to continuous innovation. The company has earned its reputation as a trusted leader by prioritizing transparency, ethical practices, and bold decision-making. Clients and partners can be confident in the leadership driving OKUNS GLOBAL's success, knowing their needs will be met with professionalism, dedication, and forward-thinking solutions.

Conclusion

As we conclude the narratives of Okunrounmu Foundation and Okuns Global Enterprises, it is evident that both entities embody a steadfast commitment to progress, resilience, and impact. From humble beginnings to becoming a multifaceted global entity, Okuns Global has not only weathered the challenges of international business but thrived by maintaining core values of integrity, innovation, and community service.

The Okunrounmu Foundation continues to give back to communities, while Okuns Global Enterprises sets new standards for business excellence across borders. This business model, rooted in purpose and driven by passion, inspires entrepreneurs, leaders, and visionaries alike.

Okuns Global Enterprises is positioned to expand, innovate in new markets, and continue fostering meaningful partnerships as we look toward the future. This chapter serves as a testimony to what can be achieved through dedicated leadership, a global mindset, and the desire to create lasting change.

VENTURE INTO A GLOBAL ENTITY

The story does not end here; it is only the beginning of even greater horizons for Okuns Global and the impact it aims to leave on the world.

A GLOBAL CALL TO ACTION TO TURN CHALLENGES INTO BOUNDLESS OPPORTUNITIES

AS I BRING THIS BOOK to a close, I am reminded of the meaning behind its title, *Venture into a Global Entity: Turn Your Adversities into Success Across Continents*. This is not just a phrase; it embodies what it takes to build something significant in today's interconnected world. We live in an era of inevitable challenges, but success lies in turning those adversities into stepping stones. Whether navigating cultural barriers, adapting to new markets, or overcoming personal setbacks, the key to lasting success is resilience, innovation, and an unwavering focus on your vision.

Venture into a Global Entity speaks to every entrepreneur or leader's ambition. It is about understanding that geography or circumstance does not limit our potential. In the modern business landscape, there are no true boundaries. What we once considered distant markets or unreachable goals are now within our grasp.

VENTURE INTO A GLOBAL ENTITY

It is about scaling your ideas beyond the local market, thinking and acting with a global mindset. The story of OKUNS GLOBAL, shared throughout this book, is a testament to how taking bold steps in uncharted waters, armed with determination and strategic thinking, can transform a local idea into a global enterprise.

Turn Your Adversities into Success Across Continents is a principle I have lived by. As I expanded my business from Nigeria to the United States and beyond, the challenges were real cultural differences, regulatory barriers, and financial limitations. But those adversities have shaped me, pushing me to become more resourceful and determined.

I encourage you, the reader, to adopt this mindset. Every challenge presents an opportunity if you choose to see it that way. Whether you are building a business, leading a team, or managing a family enterprise, the ability to transform obstacles into opportunities will set you apart in any industry or any country.

For entrepreneurs, leaders, and aspiring global citizens reading this, I urge you to think beyond the immediate, beyond the local. The lessons and insights shared here are not just a reflection of my experiences but tools for you to apply in your ventures. This book is about taking calculated risks, making informed decisions, and creating a legacy that transcends borders.

Let us turn the knowledge and insights we have explored into action by committing to growth and global excellence. Our success, our community, and the impact we make across continents depend on it.

VENTURE INTO A GLOBAL ENTITY

YOUR COMMITMENT TO GLOBAL GROWTH AND SUCCESS

I, _____,
commit to prioritizing my personal and professional growth and striving for excellence in all areas of my life. I pledge to take bold steps toward realizing my vision and expanding opportunities for myself, my family, and my community.

I will:
- ➤ Foster innovation and embrace challenges as opportunities for growth.
- ➤ Cultivate meaningful relationships that support both personal and professional success.
- ➤ Invest in my education and continuous learning to remain competitive in an ever-evolving world.
- ➤ Empower others through mentorship, sharing knowledge, and creating opportunities for collaboration.

> Take intentional action to build a legacy across borders and generations.

By taking these actions, you invest in a prosperous and impactful future. Let us turn challenges into opportunities together and build a global community where success and leadership know no boundaries.

Signature: _____

Date: _____

MOVING FORWARD WITH YOUR COMMITMENT TO GLOBAL SUCCESS

CONGRATULATIONS ON taking the first step toward building a successful and impactful future. Your commitment to personal growth, business development, and creating a legacy is a powerful move. To help you realize these ambitions, we have developed *"The Global Entrepreneur's"* training program, which is comprehensively designed to guide you through each stage of expanding your global footprint.

This program offers practical exercises, actionable strategies, and valuable insights that will equip you with the tools to navigate challenges, seize opportunities, and grow your influence across industries and continents. Additionally, you will have access to workshops, expert mentorship, and a supportive community of like-minded entrepreneurs, leaders, and professionals who share your vision.

Engaging with this program will strengthen your business acumen and leadership skills and help you gain the confidence needed to implement lasting change. Please register below and let me help you build a thriving global network, create new opportunities, and ensure you become a global entity.

Please fill out this form and send its photo to ookunrounmu@yahoo.com with "Free Coaching" In the subject line:

Full Name: _____

Email Address: _____

Home City / Town: _____

WhatsApp Number: _____

Occupation: _____

What specific support will the training program provide to help you turn your entrepreneurial vision into a thriving global enterprise?

_____
_____
_____
_____
_____

Congratulations on taking this important step toward expanding your business and leadership impact. Your next horizon awaits in the training program, where we will provide the tailored guidance and support you need to turn your vision into a global success.

ABOUT THE AUTHOR

Dr. Olajide Okunrounmu is the founder of Okuns Global. He is responsible for the overall strategic direction and management of Okuns Global.

He earned his BSc in Physiotherapy from the Prestigious University of Lagos, Nigeria, in 1987. He completed his NYSC at Sokoto University Teaching Hospital as the Supervisor in Charge. He worked briefly as a staff therapist at Obafemi Awolowo University Teaching Hospital, Ile-Ife, Oyo state, Nigeria. He emigrated to the United Kingdom- England, looking forward to advancing his career in 1988, from where he practiced in leading Hospitals in England, including Guys, St. Charles, Orsett Hospital, etc., before being recruited to the USA in 1990.

He earned his Doctorate from Utica College, Utica, New York, in 2014. He is a man of many parts, an avid reader, and a servant leader with knacks for helping people reach their highest potential.

He also serves on the boards of several private companies and non-profit organizations in the USA and Nigeria, which are too numerous to mention. He is an ex-board member of the Yoruba American Community and a member of the Chartered Society of Professional Allied to Medicine, England, the American Physical Therapy Association, and the Nigeria Society of Physiotherapy.

He is happily married to his college sweetheart, Yemisi Okunrounmu, and they are both blessed with three wonderful children and two gracious grandchildren.

www.ingramcontent.com/pod-product-compliance
Lightning Source LLC
Chambersburg PA
CBHW051646040426
42446CB00009B/1000